THE GRIZZLIES OF GLACIER

By
WARREN L. HANNA
Author Of
MONTANA'S MANY-SPLENDORED GLACIERLAND

Mountain Press Publishing Company
Missoula, Montana

Cover painting by
Robert Neaves

Library of Congress Cataloging in Publication Data

Hanna, Warren Leonard, 1898-
 The grizzlies of Glacier.

 Bibliography: p.
 Includes index.
 1. Grizzly bear. 2. Mammals — Montana — Glacier National
Park. 3. Glacier National Park. I. Title.
QL737.C27H39   599'.74446   77-23004
ISBN 0-87842-072-X

Mountain Press Publishing Company
279 West Front Street
Missoula, Montana 59801

FOREWORD

The grizzly bear has been formally declared to be a "threatened species" by federal authorities in belated recognition of the fact that complete extinction of this remarkable animal has taken place throughout most of its historic range in our lower 48 states. It is difficult to believe that the fewer than 1,000 big bears that cling to an existence in three or four of our western states are the last of more than 100,000 that roamed the area west of the Mississippi but little more than a century ago.

The grizzly, undoubtedly the most intelligent and most invincible game animal ever to inhabit this continent, if not the entire world, has been a source of deep fascination to those who have had an opportunity to study it. Because of this great interest, a rather considerable literature dealing with the big bears has come from the pens of explorers, hunters and naturalists.

From the time that the grizzly was brought to general attention by Lewis and Clark, it has been highly controversial. Different biographers have given it a variety of characterizations. The earliest of these pictured the big bears as ferocious monsters literally thirsting for human blood, creatures that hated man and seldom failed to attack or even to hunt him. They were also anathema to cattlemen of the old West whose herds had suffered from grizzly predation.

On the other hand, the grizzly has had many admirers, some of whom have regarded it with an almost euphoric affection. They have found it not to be ferocious, but rather a vigorous, courageous adventurer, excelling in mental acumen and physical prowess.

They were impressed by its bulk, agility, strength, poise and courage, all of which combined to make it a masterful fighter if forced to defend itself. One grizzly aficionado even dedicated his book on the big bears "with the respect, admiration and affection of the author to the noblest wild animal of North America, the Grizzly Bear."

To the millions of visitors to Glacier Park, the grizzly has been a chief attraction and source of interest, although not many are so fortunate as to see one in the flesh. Nevertheless, no one spends so much as a day within Park environs without being made conscious of their existence. Park authorities make sure of that. It appears, moreover, that the Park may be the one area in our lower 48 states where the grizzly is thriving, rather than fighting a losing battle for survival. The conditions there, apart from the brief but heavy flow of summer visitors, are ideal for grizzly living, and the management of the bear population on the part of the Park Service has been intelligent.

Of course, the grizzly still has its detractors who react vigorously and unfavorably to news of mishaps resulting from confrontations with the big bears. They deplore the Park's record of fatalities, unimpressed by the fact that three deaths among the nearly 30,000,000 visitors since the Park was established as such represent one in 10,000,000 - safer odds for a vacationer, as one naturalist has commented, than swimming, boating, baseball, football, or even taking a shower.

The grizzlies of Glacier National Park loom large in popular interest through their prominence in myth and legend, as well as in dramatic episodes of real life. For those who would like to know more about this colorful animal, both in the Park and in general, the chapters which follow have been prepared. Hopefully, they may provide a broader understanding of the great bears and the part which they play in the ecology of the few areas where they are still given an opportunity for survival.

TABLE OF CONTENTS

    I. Grizzly Haven..1

   II. Super Bear 13

  III. Aristocrat Of The Wilderness.............................19

  IV. Legendary Animal Of The New World 25

   V. Lewis And Clark "Discover" The Grizzly............31

  VI. How The Grizzly Got Its Names........................43

 VII. Grizzly Myths 51

VIII. Grizzlies: Aggressive Or Defensive?.....................57

  IX. Grizzlies As Pets 65

   X. Hunting The Grizzly Near Lake St. Mary.............75

  XI. The Medicine Grizzly Of Cut Bank Canyon 89

 XII. Grizzly Femmes Fatales 99

XIII. The Twin Tragedies Of 1967 117

XIV. The Park Service Grizzly Program 133

Appendix: Ecological Role And Management Of Grizzly
Bears In Glacier National Park, Montana
— C.J. Martinka 143

Looking across Swiftcurrent Lake at the Many Glacier Hotel, show place of the Rockies.

I

GRIZZLY HAVEN

Glacier National Park is one of the last strongholds of the grizzly bear. Its million acres of wilderness, its status as a sanctuary for wild life, and its combination of mountainous terrain and excellent forage make the Park a safe and inviting habitat for the big bears.

The grizzly was undoubtedly one of the pioneers in the region that is Glacier, enjoying a tenancy that has continued for centuries — how many can only be a matter of conjecture. It is reasonable to believe, however, that the big bears moved into the wooded valleys soon after the last of the great glaciers had vanished, continuing thereafter to dominate the area until the advent of the white man with his lethal weapons.

There were actually, according to bear experts, two types of grizzlies in the territory that came to be Montana. One of these, the light-colored "Big Plains Grizzly," flourished along the upper Missouri and, as a matter of fact, throughout most of the plains country west of the 100th meridian. By reason of its open habitat, its aggressive disposition, and the rapid incursion of settlers into the old West, this subspecies was relentlessly hunted to extinction before the end of the 19th century. The other, sometimes called the "Rocky Mountain Grizzly," was found in rugged areas, mostly above an elevation of 4,000 feet. Because of its elusive nature, and the character of its habitat, it has continued to survive in a few areas where it has been given a measure of protection, and to thrive in Glacier and Yellowstone Parks where it is fully protected.

Early Game Hunters

The accounts of early visitors to the future Park region made few references to its bear population, suggesting that encounters, if any, with grizzlies were rare. During the two decades commencing with

1884, many well-known personages hunted game in parts of the area which is now the Park. Among these were George Bird Grinnell, Henry L. Stimson, Emerson Hough, Ralph Pulitzer and Thomas, Robert and Cecil Baring, members of the distinguished English banking family, usually with James Willard Schultz as their guide and mentor.

The principal objectives of all these hunters were the rare Rocky Mountain goats and sheep, although they occasionally killed deer, elk and antelope. While the Grinnell party was hunting near Singleshot Mountain in 1884, they found signs of grizzlies, but actually saw none of these animals. In September, 1886, while exploring a part of the Swiftcurrent Valley, they returned to camp to find that bears (species not identified) had made off with all of their fresh meat, bacon and dried fruit, and had ripped open their sack of flour with disastrous results.

At Two Medicine Lake*

A dramatic encounter with a huge grizzly was said to have taken place in what is now the Park in 1864. This was the time when the celebrated "White Blackfoot," Hugh Monroe, had left his employment with the American Fur Company at Fort Benton. Gathering all of his children and grandchildren, as well as the necessary lodges, gear and horses, he set forth for the Two Medicine Valley. After several days' travel, they reached the shores of Two Medicine Lake, in the shadow of the great peak subsequently given Monroe's Indian name of Rising Wolf.

The cavalcade included two of Monroe's grandsons, Robert and William Jackson, aged 10 and 8 respectively. For them, the trip was a great adventure, and they were anxious to make use of the lightweight rifles which they had received as gifts the preceding Christmas, but which they had been forbidden to use unless accompanied by their father or grandfather. One day while on the trail with the grandfather, they stole away with their rifles at the ready, eagerly looking for deer and elk, fresh tracks of which they had seen.

---

*This adventure of the Jackson brothers is based on pages 13-18, inclusive, of *William Jackson, Indian Scout* by James Willard Schultz, reprinted in 1976 by William K. Cavanagh, First National Bank Building, Springfield, Illinois 62701, and adapted for use in these pages through special permission by Mr. Cavanagh.

Presently they saw the thick brush at the lower end of a small, grassy park quiver as if some kind of an animal were passing through. Because of its dark body they thought it was a buffalo, and Robert fired at it. With the report, they heard a frightful, hoarse cry of pain, and out of the brush leaped a monstrous bear, obviously a grizzly. William also fired, and saw the bear flinch as it came bounding toward them.

The two frightened youngsters fled back up the trail, yelling for help from their grandfather. William leaped for the low-hanging limb of a tree, and pulled himself up, but not before the bear had ripped his trouser leg with its claws. Just as the animal was about to spring at him again, it suddenly sank quivering to the ground as their grandfather's rifle gave a thunderous boom.

Needless to say, the grandfather gave them both a good scolding as they helped to skin the great beast which Monroe said would weigh all of a thousand pounds. His shot had broken its neck, while William's shot, although not immediately fatal, had pierced the end of one lung. Ten years later, this same William Jackson and his brother were serving as scouts with General Custer in the Black Hills, and in 1876 were with Major Reno at the time of the massacre on the Little Big Horn.

Report By A Naturalist

Seemingly, so far as the records they left are concerned, early visitors to this far corner of Montana were not particularly interested in members of the bear family.* However, before the turn of the century, the future Park was visited by the eminent naturalist, Vernon Bailey, who reported that in the spring and early summer of 1895, grizzlies were the commonest bears of the St. Mary area. He told of seeing several of them in May and June of that year, and commented that "throughout the forest in this region bear tracks, beds and signs were abundant at the lower levels."

After revisiting the same area more than 20 years later, he prepared a report which included much information on the status of the

---

*For a notable exception to this statement, see Chapter 10, infra, relating the story of a hunter's fascinating adventures with Montana grizzlies — a story which, until now, has escaped general attention because its well-known author chose to have it privately printed for distribution to his friends only.

grizzly population as he had found it during the latter part of the 19th century. Especially interesting were the following comments:

From the early eighties to the time when Glacier Park was created in 1910, this was one of the most popular regions for hunting bears in the whole United States, and many were killed each year by sportsmen, and others were caught by the numerous trappers of the region. In 1895 I found lines of bear traps between Summit and Belton up to late in June. Even then some of the trappers who were thoroughly familiar with the methods of killing large game for bear bait considered bear trapping the greatest menace to the game of the region. Traps were baited with mountain sheep, goats and deer, and I was told that at least 500 elk and moose were killed every year for bear bait. Most of the trapping was done in spring, when the bears first came out of hibernation and the fur was at its longest and best. As they enter their dens for the winter hibernation with the first cold weather and deep snows, usually in late October or early November, and do not reappear until early in April, the time for securing their skins in prime condition is short at either end of the season.

Early Game Protection

Steps to provide a measure of protection for wildlife of the region were first taken in 1897 when it became part of the Lewis and Clark Forest Reserve created at that time. Nevertheless, enforcement was minimal and hunting and trapping continued to flourish, especially in remote valleys, not to mention forays by Cree Indians of Canada into the Kintla Lake country. A more active program of protection was undertaken in 1902 and by 1925 was paying substantial dividends. The intervening years had done wonders toward increasing the numbers of wild animals within the Park, including bears, as well as toward stocking adjacent districts with game for the benefit of hunters.

The number of grizzlies within Park boundaries at the present time is estimated at 200. Since the area of the Park embraces more than 1500 square miles, this provides a theoretical range of 7 to 8 square miles for each bear. Having in mind that a substantial percentage of the total would be mother bears with two cubs each, the average range for adult grizzlies might be as much as 10 to 12 square miles apiece.

Visitors and Park personnel are asked to report sightings of all bears within Park boundaries, and these records suggest that as many as 5 or 6 per week may be glimpsed during the regular travel season. Where the encounters or sightings are along frequented trails, it has been a practice to close the latter until the possibility of danger seems to have been dissipated. Consequently, most visitors, particularly those who do little hiking, never catch a glimpse of a grizzly.

Former "Show-time" At Big Hotels

This has not always been the case, however. In the Park's earlier years, when the hotels and chalets were new, it was customary, following a long-established practice in Yellowstone Park, to have a garbage dump at a convenient distance from the hotel kitchen. These were soon discovered by bears of all species and their feeding at various dumps became an evening spectacle, often watched at a respectful distance by visitors and hotel employees. Particularly was this the case at Many Glacier Hotel and at Lake McDonald Lodge, then called Lewis's Hotel. When grizzlies put in an appearance, smaller black bears usually made themselves scarce.

Although garbage dumps thus gave many visitors a chance to see grizzlies at fairly close range, they have since been abolished in both parks. The enticing dumps caused the animals to lose their natural fear of man, and to be attracted to those parts of the Park frequented by man with correspondingly increased danger of injury and accident. Now hotel garbage is disposed of in such a way as to obviate any bear problem, and even garbage cans placed throughout the Park for visitor use are now bear-proof.

Rogue Bears Create Problems

Some bear's stray across the invisible Park boundaries from time to time, into areas where they are not protected by Park regulations, and where there are privately owned habitations, including summer homes and small ranches with pets and livestock. These folks, living mostly along the North and Middle Forks of the Flathead River near the Park boundaries, are subject to state game laws and federal statutes pertaining to "threatened species." They are sometimes put in an awkward position when a visiting grizzly makes a nuisance of itself on their premises, and they must act in defense of their property.

Not long ago such a situation arose on the North Fork of the Flathead River (but outside the Park) when a young grizzly raided some outbuildings of a small rancher and killed a calf. The rancher, attracted by the commotion, got his gun and shot the grizzly. Dutifully he reported the incident to the authorities, only to be rewarded by being arrested and having to pay a fine for killing the bear without a permit and out of season.

Others are less conscientious under such circumstances, and at least one householder along the Middle Fork has risen to the defense of his home when a rogue grizzly undertook to "break and enter" through the front door. The animal's pelt now graces his living room floor. A year later his wife, about to drive to Kalispell for a medical appointment, was kept housebound for more than three hours by a young grizzly meandering about the front yard. The owners had set up a gazebo, placing within it an old kitchen range which they planned to use for barbecues. Before they had a chance to do so, however, a visiting grizzly invaded the gazebo and with a few well directed swipes of its powerful paws demolished the range completely.

Vandalism Within The Park

Official Park property has not always been free from damage by the big bears. In the spring of 1941, Park authorities erected directional signs along the Camas Lake trail to provide assistance to hikers and trail riders in finding their way through the wilderness. Not long after their erection, several signs were found broken and lying on the ground. Claw and tooth marks provided unmistakable evidence that the saboteur was a bear that apparently resented man's intrusion in an area once controlled by members of the animal kingdom alone.

Similarly, there has been occasional damage to property of Park concessioners. In the early 1930's, while chalets at Going-To-The-Sun Camp on Lake St. Mary were still in use, one of the cottages had been boarded up for the winter at the end of the travel season. A grizzly broke in through a window, smashing not only that window, but the other nine, all of the latter from the inside. In each case the glass had been pounded into fine bits, as well as the porcelain dishware; even the iron stove was broken into pieces. To put an artistic touch on the whole thing, the bear found a sack of flour, in which it punched several holes, and then sprinkled it finely over the whole wreck.

For some years it has been Park Service practice to tranquilize and transport any bear that becomes a nuisance to a remote part of the Park where it is released, hopefully to find a new life, free from vandalism or other problem-causing tendencies. Since results of this operation have been something less than 100% successful, other methods of handling may be under consideration.

The Grizzly From Giefer Creek

One example of this kind of handling occurred during the summer of 1976. Newspapers of the Glacier Park area carried many items about a grizzly which had been causing trouble in the vicinity of Giefer Creek, a few miles west of Marias Pass but just outside Park boundaries. It had originally been trapped in the summer of 1975 and transferred to a new location on the South Fork of the Flathead River. Before long, however, it returned to its old haunts on Giefer Creek, where it was trapped again in 1976. This time a radio-tracking collar was attached and the bear was released at the upper end of Whale Creek on the North Fork of the Flathead.

The grizzly soon moved to a part of the North Fork area near the Canadian border and, as of early August, 1976, was reported to have broken into 19 cabins, some of them twice. Unsuccessful efforts were then made to trap it again with a view to transporting it to Fort Churchill, near Hudson Bay, where the Canadian Wildlife Service has a large laboratory.

After September, however, nothing more was heard from the bear until April 24, 1977 when it was killed on Wigwam Creek in British Columbia, some 15 miles north of the border, by Ray Koontz of McConnellsburg, Pennsylvania. With the aid of Thomas Kogler, a guide and outfitter of Cranbrook, B.C., Koontz had packed in and hunted for three days before seeing the big grizzly. It was identified by the tags placed on its ears when captured in previous years. It had made an unknowing but fatal error in wandering from the United

The grizzly from Giefer Creek as it looks today. Pictured with the bear is Ray Koontz who killed it in British Columbia on April 24, 1977.

States where, as a member of a "threatened species," it had protection, into a part of Canada where it was not against the law to hunt or kill a grizzly.

Other Grizzlies Of The Park's 1976 Season

With several thousand visitors passing through the Park each day of the rather brief season, some encounters with the area's 200-odd grizzlies are bound to occur. These are infrequent and injuries are rare, although results vary from season to season. 1976, for example, was a season with more than the average number of incidents, all of them scary. Twenty-one people were involved in a total of seven incidents during July, August and September. Of the twenty-one, five gained safety by climbing trees, four by fleeing into a nearby lake, and four by leaving the trail. Of the others, six were not obliged to take evasive action because not personally attacked, while four sustained injuries, one of which proved fatal.

July 16th: At 8:30 a.m., two young California men were asleep in their sleeping bags in a tent at the Middle Campsite at Logging Lake when a young grizzly sat against one side of their tent. Noting that there seemed to be movement within the tent, he bit through the canvas and into the left shoulder of one of the occupants, causing superficial wounds. When the men ran out of the tent, the bear chased them (they were unclothed) into the chilly lake where it held them off shore for about an hour before departing.

July 19th: At about dusk, a grizzly with two cubs ran through the tent of three young hikers who were camped illegally at Hidden Lake. They were forced to pick up their gear as best they could and retreat toward the Logan Pass Visitor Center. There they were discovered about midnight by a patrol ranger and were given citations for camping without a permit. None of them was injured.

August 10th: Four hikers traveling along the Highline trail (Granite Park to Logan Pass) saw a small grizzly coming toward them on the trail. They retreated, and when the bear kept coming, they dropped an occasional sandwich which it would pause to eat. When it still kept coming, they went below the trail, passing in and out of fog, and saw no more of the bear.

August 15th: Two teenage girls, visiting from Minneapolis, were hiking toward Iceberg Lake. They saw a grizzly following them and commenced to walk faster, but the bear also moved faster. Finally they dropped their backpacks and climbed nearby trees. The bear stood on its hind legs below the trees and growled, but after a little while went up the mountainside. It had not bothered their backpacks.

September 9th: In the late afternoon, Roscoe Black, manager of the St. Mary Village facilities, located at the east end of the Going-To-The-Sun Highway, together with two female members of the St. Mary dining room staff, were hiking down the switchbacks from Stoney Indian Pass on the way to Goathaunt at the American end of Waterton Lake. Unexpectedly, a young grizzly, weighing 200 to 250 pounds, charged onto the trail and inflicted serious lacerations upon Black and one of the young ladies, causing immediate incapacity to both. The other young woman went for help, and the injured pair were evacuated that evening by helicopter to Kalispell where they spent several days in the hospital.

September 19th: Early on a Sunday afternoon two Montana State University students were fishing at Fishercap Lake, not far from the Many Glacier Campground, when two young grizzlies appeared, one of them rather aggressive. They caused one of the men to flee into the lake to escape attack, while his companion climbed a tree. The aggressive bear pursued the first man into the lake, but was frightened off by his yells. As soon as the situation permitted, the men swam to the foot of the lake and reported the matter to the Many Glacier Ranger Station. Neither had been physically injured.

September 23rd: At 6:30 a.m. a young grizzly invaded a tent at the Many Glacier Campground, where three University of Montana coeds were in their sleeping bags. It dragged one of them, sleeping bag and all, out of the tent to a distance of 300 yards away where, after being badly mauled, she was killed. Two young men who volunteered to guard the body were forced to climb trees when the grizzly returned to the scene unexpectedly. Rangers then shot the killer bear and its companion, which had put in a belated appearance. Both were two or three years old and weighed about 250 pounds each. It would appear that these were the same two bears that had caused the problem at Fishercap Lake the preceding Sunday.

Problems Of Bear Management

No two incidents are identical, of course, and some of these which have been described are not really typical, since grizzly invasions of campers' tents in Glacier Park are practically unheard of; and the fatality was only the third in all of the Park's history.

Each incident or encounter presents a difficult situation for all concerned, with the ever-present possibility of injury to be considered. Consequently, each episode is given careful and immediate attention by the Park's bear management authorities, who then take prompt steps to close the trail where the encounter took place, or to institute other indicated measures. An aggressive campaign is constantly waged by officials to make visitors realize that all bears can be dangerous, and to help them know how to avert possible trouble when it appears.

Since 1967, in recognition of the unique problem posed by Glacier's bears, the National Park Service has provided the Park with a research biologist to conduct ecological studies of the grizzly and certain other animals. This specialist has made an intensive study of the subject, and the resulting program for bear management is considered by authorities in the field to be the most effective in the national park system. Although entitled to an "excellent" rating, it is, as the Park's 1976 record shows, still something less than perfect.

Overlooking Helen Lake in the scenic Belly River country.

II

SUPER BEAR

The grizzly is unquestionably the most powerful wild beast in the Western hemisphere; indeed, it is the largest carnivore, or flesh-eating mammal, in the entire world. With its robust body and sturdy legs, the grizzly is not only a much larger and heavier animal, but also a more formidable one than the common black bear with which most people are familiar.

As a matter of fact, it is only through a comparison of the two species that the magnitude of this extraordinary creature can be fully appreciated. It was Lewis and Clark who first made this comparison in their journal of 1804-1806, laying stress upon the grizzly's unusual dimensions, the size of its feet and claws, its fearlessness, its remarkable tenacity of life, and the peculiarity of its scrotum. They also noted that a grizzly's fur is much finer, thicker and deeper than that of the black bear, and that its legs, talons and tusks are of greater length.

Other interesting differences, largely of a behavioral character, have been pointed out by Enos Mills:*

> The grizzly is energetic, thorough, works hard, and takes life rather seriously; while the black bear is lazy, careless, does no more work each day than is necessary, and is more playful. The grizzly's hibernating-den is usually a substantial, complete affair, while that of the black bear is more or less of a makeshift. The black bear likes to play with other bears, while the grizzly enjoys playing alone. The black climbs a tree easily and often sleeps in a tree-top; the grizzly bear rarely climbs after he passes cubhood.

---

*The Grizzly, Our Greatest Wild Animal, published in 1919 by Houghton Mifflin Company.

Head And Shoulders

In relation to the rest of its body, the grizzly's head is proportionately small and rather acutely tapered, with less length of snout and greater over-all bulk toward the base of the skull, because of the powerful jaw muscles. Its profile is often described as "dished-in," while that of the black bear is straight. The grizzly has piercing black eyes, set wide apart, but rather small in comparison with those of other large animals. The ears are short. The normal adult has 42 teeth, so shaped and placed as to facilitate its feeding upon both flesh and plant food, including fangs or tusks (canine teeth) which may reach a length of 2½ inches and are useful for tearing, gripping and holding.

A characteristic feature of the grizzly is the hump on its shoulders, which is attributable to the size and placement of the muscles above the shoulder blades. This higher shoulder area, like the hump on the buffalo or on a Rocky Mountain goat, makes the grizzly readily identifiable, even at a distance.

In comparison with that of many animals of the forest, the vision of the grizzly is poor; and it lacks the acute sense of hearing of deer, for example. However, it possesses an exceptionally keen sense of smell which serves it well in dealing with wild life generally, as well as with man. Ordinarily, the grizzly is a rather silent animal, except when wounded or seriously disturbed. At such times, it may emit a tremendous roar, but such sounds as it otherwise makes may be described as a growl, grunt, sniff, snarl or woofing noise.

Coat And Coloring

The pelage of the grizzly consists of an underfur which constitutes a fine, thick fleece lining, together with coarser and longer guard hairs that project from it. These protruding hairs often have a silverish tip. Commonly the fur is long and shaggy on the grizzly's flanks and shoulders, although it may appear somewhat unkempt or "mangy" when the coat is far worn or the animal is thin. The annual molt, which comes in late summer or in autumn, gives the bear a new coat with more insulation for the winter and hibernal period.

The grizzly's coat is more varied in coloration than that of many other kinds of mammals. The color of the species ranges from dark to light, from a near black to the near white of the plains grizzly. In Montana, most of the specimens seen or killed are brown, but the animal can be light or dark brown, tan, gray, or even cinnamon-colored. In fact, because of this wide variation in coloring, Lewis and Clark were puzzled as to whether all belonged to one species, and finally commented that the animal "might well be termed the variegated bear."

Donald Stevenson, who lived for many years on Swiftcurrent Creek around the turn of the century, became very familiar with the grizzlies of the area since his primary occupation was that of hunter and trapper. Some of them, he reported, "were nearly black in color, with white tips to the hairs of the face and sides, some were a rusty brown, while others were a golden yellow along the sides."

General Physique

The grizzly has a substantial look, his massive proportions suggesting strength rather than bulk. With back broad and well-rounded, and feet pulled well together beneath him, he may at first appearance seem top-heavy. But this impression is dissipated the moment his movements display his ease of adjustment and nicety of balance. He has an abbreviated tail, but it is the only insignificant thing about him.

Like man, the grizzly is a plantigrade or flat-footed animal, with five well-developed toes on each foot. The hind feet are larger, the tracks of adult animals measuring up to 13 inches in length and seven inches across the toes. Though shorter, the tracks of the fore feet generally show five distinct claw prints.

The front claws of adult grizzlies range from four to six inches in length, are usually curved, and in some cases are twice as long as those on the back feet. They serve the big bears well in their extensive digging operations for bulbs, roots and rodents, as well as in fighting. Many human beings have been deeply gashed by these great hooks that are powered by heavy arm and shoulder muscles. The claws are also essential when the grizzly prepares a bedroom for the winter.

After many months of strenuous use in mountainous terrain, the grizzly's fore claws lose some of their length and curvature. During the long hibernal sleep, however, the worn-down claws have a chance to regenerate, and by spring are again long and pointed.

Size And Weight

The grizzly is of heroic size and build. When an adult grizzly rises on its hind legs to its full stature, it is indeed a formidable and frightening beast, standing eight to ten feet in height. This makes it possible to obtain fruit, nuts and other food beyond the reach of ordinary mammals, and also to get at hunters and others seeking refuge in small trees. In a prone position, a full-grown grizzly will usually measure six to seven feet from nose to tail. In a normal standing position, it is somewhere between three and four feet tall at the shoulder.

At birth cubs weigh between ten and twenty ounces, each being about the size of a chipmunk. In proportion to the size of the mother, the grizzly is one of the smallest animals at birth, its weight representing about one-fifth of one per cent of that of the mother. If the cubs were much larger, it would be impossible for the mother to nourish them during the hibernal period when she has been neither eating nor drinking for a few months. Growth is rapid, however, and the average weight at six months is fifty pounds.

The grizzly always appears larger than it really is, and the weight of any individual naturally depends upon its age, sex, state of health and nutrition, and possibly the season of the year. A fully grown animal may weigh in excess of 1,000 pounds, but the average is probably less than 500 pounds. Males weigh about one-fourth more than females.

Speed And Strength

The stride of a grizzly varies with the size of the animal and the degree of its haste, but the average is between 21 and 28 inches. When running rapidly, these distances may increase to as much as eight feet. Although it appears to move with a lumbering gait, its speed over rough terrain is remarkable. It can outrun a man and, for a short distance, is said to be able to equal the speed of a horse. Its gait at top speed is a gallop, although at lesser speeds it is an easy, ground-covering, bounding lope that can readily be maintained over all types of terrain.

The grizzly is an animal of extraordinary strength. It has been known to drag the carcass of a cow or of an elk of perhaps twice its own weight to a place where it would prefer to eat it or to cache it away. Sometimes this will involve moving it up a mountainside and over fallen logs. With its powerful paws, it has on more than one occasion broken the back of a steer or other large animal with a single blow. In describing this feature of the species, Enos Mills commented:

> The grizzly is exceptionally expert and agile with his paws. With either fore paw he can strike like a sledge-hammer or lift a heavy weight. He boxes or strikes with lightning-like rapidity. Most grizzlies are right-handed, that is, the right paw is most used. If a small object is to be touched or moved, he will daintily use but one claw.

Cubhood And Maturity

Grizzly litters are usually comprised of two cubs, with a maximum of four. They rarely weigh much over a pound at birth, and are born in January or early February in the den, the eyes not yet open, toothless, and naked except for a fine, short gray hair. At that time, the entrance to the winter den, usually situated at a high elevation, may be blanketed by several feet of snow. The cubs continue to nurse from the mother throughout the remainder of the hibernal period and sometimes until the age of seven months.

Litters of young grizzlies accompany their mothers for one or two years, and it is only when the maternal bond is broken that she will breed again. This means that mating takes place every second or third summer. The gestation period is about 180 days. While cubs may den up together for their second winter, adult grizzlies never spend the winter in the same den. Nor do adults ordinarily travel together in a group, although males and females may consort for a time during the mating season.

The grizzly reaches sexual maturity at about 3½ years of age. A minimum of six years is required for the attainment of full stature and weight, although experts believe that complete maturity of free bears is not ordinarily reached in less than eight years. A five-year-old may appear full-grown, but in the wild state may continue to develop in size and weight for another three to five years.

Longevity And Death

The age to which the wild grizzly may live is largely a matter of conjecture. Because of its few real enemies in a protected wilderness, it would seem that only the physical forces of nature, disease, or old age could bring about death. The grizzly, of course, is subject to accident and members of the species are the occasional victims of forest fire, snowslide and falling rock. One or two have been found frozen to death while hibernating during an extremely cold winter. Yet death from natural causes is evidently the lot of most wild grizzlies, despite the fact that only rarely, according to experts, have the remains of such animals been found.

Such zoo records as are available on the longevity of captive grizzlies indicate a life span of 20 to 25 years in most cases, with none surviving beyond age 30. However, conditions of food and confinement are so different from those in the animal's normal environment that such statistics are meaningless as a basis for estimating the probable longevity of wild bears. Experts have considered that, under favorable circumstances, free grizzlies may live from 25 to 40 years. Enos Mills believed that their normal life span was probably from 35 to 50 years.

III

ARISTOCRAT OF THE WILDERNESS

Of all the wild creatures inhabiting the western half of North America in pioneer days, three were of surpassing interest. These were the beaver, the buffalo and the grizzly bear.

The reasons for this popular interest were not difficult to divine. In the case of the beaver, it was the value of its pelt. In reference to the buffalo, it was attributable to its size, the superiority of its flesh, and the ease with which its hides were converted into robes. As for the grizzly, it was by reason of its boldness, its prodigious strength, and its awesome appearance.

Those who knew the grizzly best were its greatest admirers. John Muir applied the term "the sequoia of the animals" to the grizzlies that once inhabited the Yosemite Valley. Theodore Roosevelt referred to the grizzly as "the King of Game Animals of temperate North America." James Capen Adams, whose experience in the world of the grizzly was nothing if not unique, described it as —

> ...the monarch of American beasts and, in many respects, the most formidable animal in the world to be encountered. In comparison with the lion of Africa and the tiger of Asia, though these may exhibit more activity and bloodthirstiness, the grizzly is not second in courage and excels them in power.* Like the regions which he inhabits, there is a vastness in his strength which makes him a fit companion for the monster trees and rocks of the Sierra, and places him, if not the first, at least in the first rank of all quadrupeds.

---

*A projected battle between *Parnell,* a 650-pound lion, and *Siskiyou,* an 850-pound grizzly, on April 28, 1894, at Col. Dan'l Boone's Arena at the San Francisco Midwinter Fair of that year was prevented by authorities from taking place on the grounds of cruelty to animals. *Parnell* had killed one of his keepers, Carlo Thieman, at that same location on February 13, 1894.

Sagacity And Dignity

Grizzly experts have always been impressed with the intelligence of the animal. Enos Mills left no doubt about his opinion on the subject:

> I would give the grizzly first place in the animal world for brain-power. He is superior in mentality to the horse, the dog, and even the gray wolf. Instinct the grizzly has, but he also has the ability to reason. His ever-alert, amazingly developed senses are constantly supplying his brain with information — information which he uses and uses intelligently.

Theodore Roosevelt considered the grizzly to be a "shrewd beast" with an "unusual bear-like capacity for adapting himself to changed conditions" — an adaptability that converted him from a bold to a wary animal as waves of settlers overran the territory over which he used to reign.

Along with his sagacity, the grizzly has a composure and equanimity not possessed by lesser members of the animal kingdom. In his movements are a certain grace and dignity, a lordliness of carriage, and an indifference to all the world that have been remarked by observers of wild life.

This same poise and dignity, for example, were noted by John Muir in chance encounters with bears in the Yosemite Valley. On one of these occasions, he came upon a formidable-appearing grizzly which caught sight of him as he tried to hide behind a nearby cedar, stared sharply for a minute or two, and then, as Muir described it, "with fine dignity disappeared in a manzanita-covered earthquake talus."

Territorial Imperative

As is the case with many wild creatures, an adult grizzly has his own home territory, over which he claims the right of exclusive use. Because of his size and needs, the bear is likely to hold a larger territory than may be claimed by other species — the mountain lion, beaver or eagle, for example. Regardless, however, of the extent to which there may be a conflict with the territories of lesser species, the grizzly will dominate the scene. He will brook no interference by others within his home territory; there he makes his living, and in it he commonly dies.

Topography, mountain barriers, streams and other natural boundaries are all factors in determining the form of a grizzly's home territory. The size is determined by the food supply, by the bear population of the region, and by individual prowess. Finding its own home range when its mother unties the apron strings can be as much of an adventure for the young bear as for the young human. And it can prove just as frustrating for the bear, as for the human, when the opportunities for adolescent expansion into a seemingly bright new world turn out to have been preempted by others.

Within his home territory, when he acquires one, the grizzly leads a solitary life. Alone he hunts for food, wanders for adventure, fights his foes, if any, and in solitude dens up in winter. Because of his strong attachment to his home territory, he seldom leaves it; but a scarcity of food may cause him to do so temporarily, or excessive food elsewhere may attract him.

Day To Day Routine

The grizzly spends most of his waking hours making a living. He has a prodigious appetite and, because his taste runs to small types of food, mostly vegetarian, he must keep on the move. He digs up roots, feeds on tender shoots of shrubbery, seeds, pine-nuts and berries; he eats bark like a rabbit and grass like a grass-eater. He is skilled in locating grubs that live under logs and rocks, and in making the contents of a well-populated ant-hill available for consumption. Not infrequently he will evacuate sizeable holes in the terrain digging out a ground squirrel from its burrow, a rather small morsel for a great deal of work.

Grizzlies are fond of fish and are usually rather adept fishermen. Sometimes they will wade up shallow streams, seizing with claws or teeth the fish that conceal themselves beneath banks and projecting roots. Sometimes the bear will deftly knock them out of the water and onto the bank with a quick flip of the paw. In Glacier Park the Kokanee salmon spawn in and about the confluence of the Middle and North Forks of the Flathead River, providing a series of field days for the bears of that area.

The grizzly has not, as a general rule, been a killer of big game. In parts of the country where there are plenty of elk and deer, he is willing to include them in his menu — if they have been winter-killed or have met death in some other way — and the same is true as to cattle and sheep. Except in rare cases, the grizzly declines to do his own butchering.

Foods And Feeding

Being an omnivore, the grizzly enjoys foods of many kinds and, as some one has said, he is a walking garbage can. To a certain extent, his foraging is determined by the calendar and he feeds on whatever the season affords. He knows when each article of diet is in season and where, in his home territory or out of it, this abounds.

A study of the spring diet of the grizzlies of Glacier has shown a predominance of plants, grasses and young green shoots, including more horsetail and cow parsnip in late May and June. Elk and deer, usually in the form of winter-killed carcasses, comprise a substantial part of the spring diet; while still another part of the food at this time of year consists of insects, principally beetles.

In summer, herbaceous items are supplemented with fruits, roots, sedges and insects, including ants. Bulbs, particularly those of the glacier lily, become a more prominent part of the menu in summer, followed by huckleberries and serviceberries as those delicacies ripen.

During autumn, huckleberries are the principal fruit eaten, supplemented by serviceberries, hawthorne and mountain ash, together with various roots and grasses. Salmon are available in some streams, and the grizzly will dig out meadow mice, pocket gophers, hibernating marmots and ground squirrels. Often it will turn over rocks and stones in search of insects and their larvae. Healthy adult animals are seldom attacked by the grizzly, although it may pounce upon stragglers, and will feed upon the bodies of such animals as it may find dead.

Preparing For Hibernation

When their respective biological clocks are triggered by the early snows and chilling temperatures of late autumn, grizzlies head for winter quarters, just as generations of bears have done for countless centuries. It may be sometime in November, or perhaps a little later, depending upon the locality and weather conditions. They become rather restless just before denning up, and frequently prepare their bedrooms in advance in order to have them ready at the psychological moment.

Their hibernal sites are usually at higher elevations, often in natural caves near timberline. Occasionally they are the handiwork of the bears themselves, accomplished through excavation under a huge rock, or hollowed out at the base of a large tree, with the entrance located between thick, steeply descending roots. Such an operation may involve the removal of as much as 300 cubic feet of soil. The nest may be lined with evergreen boughs or anything else that can be dragged in to make a bed.

When about to go into hibernation, grizzlies sometimes sleep for a day or so and then come out to wander around a bit. A change to mild weather may bring them out; but usually, when they go into their private sleeping chambers, their drowsy condition increases, and the ultimate lethargy becomes more and more profound.

The Long Winter Sleep

Actually, bears do not hibernate in the truest sense. That is, they exhibit no striking drop in body temperature with an accompanying marked decrease in breathing and pulse rate. They do go into a dormant state but maintain a temperature considerably above that of their environment. It is in this condition that the sows give birth to their young midway through the period of their long naps.

During this lengthy hibernal period, sometimes lasting up to seven months, the grizzly may remain in its winter den without coming out or tasting any food or liquid whatever. It simply subsists on the surplus fat stored up in its body, which is assimilated into its system to provide the fuel for life, as natural necessity requires it. The deep layers of fat on the outside of its body also provide an extra blanket to keep it warm, and it lapses into a lethargic state of semi-consciousness to reduce the fuel requirements. Compare this feat with man's ability to survive under similar conditions. Were he to be without food or water for but a fraction of seven months, his kidneys would shut down and produce quick disaster.

Grizzlies emerge from their winter dens between the middle of

March and the early part of May, depending upon the locality and the sex of the animals. Male bears and females without cubs leave their dens from one to three weeks before the female with cubs emerges; how the brutes can tell when to do so is one of their own secrets. Apparently it is not the melting of snows that arouses them from their winter sleep. Some small signal forever lost to man again trips a delicate interior alarm clock and informs the bears that it is time to get up.

Range Covered

Grizzlies follow no identical pattern in reference to the extent of their mobility. Radio-tracking in Yellowstone Park established that during a single week, one old male rambled over a hundred miles and swam the Yellowstone River twice. Other checks showed that many animals moved over no more than 10 or 12 square miles during the same period. It is well-known that bears which have been airlifted out of an area where they have been causing trouble often do not have too much difficulty finding their way back to familiar haunts within a short period of time.

In early days when territory was unlimited, the grizzly ranged over most of the country west of the 100th meridian to the Pacific Coast, and from Alaska south to the vicinity of Mexico City. It roamed the Rockies, the Cascades and the Sierra Nevadas. It was found as far east as the Dakotas, western Nebraska and parts of Kansas, and throughout a total of seventeen of our forty-eight lower continental states.

Today the grizzly is extinct in all but a small portion of this former range. South of the Canadian border, it no longer exists except in a few isolated areas, including two of our national parks. To be specific, it is found in Montana, Idaho and Wyoming. There may still be a few left in Colorado and Washington, but this is doubtful. Glacier and Yellowstone Parks, being nationally protected game preserves, are the principal habitats of the 700 or 800 grizzlies that remain out of an original population that has been estimated to number more than 100,000.

IV

LEGENDARY ANIMAL
OF THE NEW WORLD

Although lions and tigers have been known to our civilization for thousands of years, the American grizzly is a comparative new-comer to the pages of history. Authentic knowledge of the great bears, so far as the English-speaking world is concerned, dates from the beginning of the 19th century. Information about the species did not exist anywhere in the civilized world prior to the 17th century.

A surprising number of Europeans, or persons of European descent, found their way to the American West during the 17th and 18th centuries. They included explorers, trappers and fur traders, as well as missionaries bent on saving the souls of the country's native inhabitants. Some of these visitors kept a careful diary of their experiences, usually not published until two or three centuries later. Others arranged for contemporary publication of their adventures, including a reference, in some cases, to the fierce bears of the New World.

The travel books which followed discovery of the Americas were often factually inaccurate and sometimes purely fictional. It is not surprising that readers of the Gulliver era, with its imaginative yarns about Lilliputians and Brobdingnagians, may not have been overly impressed by occasional reports of mammoth mankilling bears in America.

The Discovery Of A Species

Grizzly bears first came to the attention of Europeans, so far as records are concerned, when Captain Sebastian Vizcaino and his crew visited the Bay of Monterey in December, 1602. Father Ascension, official diarist for the expedition, reported that large bears

25

came down to the shore at night to feed upon the carcass of a whale which had washed ashore, and that their impressive tracks measured "a good third of a yard long and a hand wide." While the term "grizzly" was then unknown, it is evident that these animals could only have been members of that species in view of the measurements given, and the fact that black bears were not native to the area.

It was more than 160 years before Spanish representatives undertook to re-visit Alta California, the first of a series of expeditions being headed by Gaspar de Portola in 1769. During the period between September 2nd and January 1, 1770, several bears were killed, according to the diary of an expedition member. Thirty more were killed by troops under the command of Lieutenant Fages near San Luis Obispo during the summer of 1771; and the Anza expedition of 1776 killed still another in the hills near San Francisco on March 29th. Father Font, diarist for the latter expedition, wrote:

> I measured this animal and he was nine spans (over six feet) long and four high. He was horrible, fierce, large and fat, and very tough. Several bullets which they fired at him when he fled they found between his hide and his flesh...

The reports of these Spanish diarists had no general circulation, however, and it remained for explorers of the Canadian sector during the 17th and 18th centuries to bring their information concerning the big bears, such as it was, to the attention of the world at large. The term "grizzly" was never applied to the California bears until after English-speaking people had taken over and the state had become a part of the union in 1850.*

Seventeenth Century Reports

Perhaps the earliest mention of unusual Canadian bears was contained in the journal of an early Jesuit missionary named Claude Jean Allouez, who got it from Indians encountered by him in an area

---

*For example, Capron in his *California: Its History,* published in 1854, says:

"THE GRIZZLY BEAR. This is the monarch of the forests. Specimens are often met which are five feet long and will weigh from 500 to 1000 pounds. This animal is of a dusky brown color, is solitary in its habits, never climbs trees, and is very powerful; but it seldom attacks man."

north of the present Assinboine River in Canada. In his "Mission to the Kilistinouc," under date of 1666, he tells of —

> ...another nation [of Indians] adjoining the Assinipoulac, who eat human beings, and live on raw fish; but these people, in turn, are eaten by bears of frightful size, all red, and with prodigiously long claws.

This may have been no more than an Indian legend, perhaps a part of tribal folklore. It may even have been a garbled understanding of what he had been told, but the area described (near Lake Winnipeg) is known to have been a grizzly habitat at one time, and the animals described sound very much like grizzly bears.

Not surprisingly, our earliest information about the grizzly from an English source was provided by an employee of the Hudson's Bay Company. The original charter of that Company had been signed on May 16, 1669 by Charles II, King of England, granting or purporting to grant to his cousin, Prince Rupert, and 17 other gentlemen, virtually sovereign powers over the vast portion of North America drained by streams entering Hudson Bay. Included in the grant were all trading, fishery, navigation and mineral rights in Rupert's Land, as the territory thus granted was referred to in the charter. It included the northeasterly portion of what is now Glacier National Park.

In the year 1690, the Company dispatched a young employee named Henry Kelsey to York Fort on Hudson Bay, from which point he undertook a two-year series of explorations extending as far as the present province of Saskatchewan and the country of the Assiniboines, with its buffalo, grizzly bears and abundance of beaver. He kept a journal of his travels, only rediscovered in 1926, which, under date of August 20, 1691, contained an entry concerning —

> ...a great sort of Bear which is Bigger than any white Bear & is neither white nor Black But silver hair'd like our English Rabbit.

First Mention Of The "Grizzled Bear"

Other early reports about the grizzlies of the Northwest were equally fragmentary, such as the comment of Baron Lahontan in his 1703 volume entitled "Memoir on the Fur-Trade in Canada" as follows:

> The reddish Bears are mischievous Creatures, for they fall fiercely upon the Huntsmen, whereas the black ones fly from 'em.

Somewhat more informative was the report of Samuel Hearne, the English explorer, whose journal covering his 1769-1772 journey across northwestern Canada stated that he —

> ...saw the skin of an enormous grizzled Bear at the tents of the Esquimaux at the Coppermine River; and many of them are said to breed not very remote from that part.

In his journal for July, 1771, while on the Coppermine River, Hearne also stated:

> The place where we lay that night is not far from Grizzled Bear Hill; which takes its name from the number of those animals that are frequently known to resort thither for the purpose of bringing forth their young in a cave that is found there.... (I saw) many hills and dry ridges on the East side of the march which were turned over like ploughed land by these animals, in searching for ground squirrels, perhaps mice, which constitute a favorite part of their food. It is surprising to see the extent of their researches in quest of these animals, and still more to view the enormous stones rolled out of their beds by the bears on those occasions.

Other Eighteenth Century Reports

According to Harold McCracken,* the work of Thomas Pennant published in 1784 and entitled "Arctic Zoology," was based upon information in reference to bears derived from several sources, including the *Journal Of a Voyage to North America* by Pierre de Charlevoix, a French Jesuit who explored along the Great Lakes and Mississippi River in 1720-1722. It was Pennant, an Englishman, who, if not the first, was at least one of the first naturalists to specifically designate the American "grizzly bear" as a separate species and to refer to it by that name.

---

*Author of the authoritative book on the grizzly entitled *The Beast That Walks Like Man.*

28

Subsequent to this identification by Pennant, another important early report on the grizzly was contributed by Edward Umfreville in his 1790 account of his 1783-1787 travels in the area west of Hudson Bay. In respect to the wildlife of that region, and with particular reference to bears, he wrote:

Bears are of three kinds: the black, the red, and the grizzle bear. The former is the least offensive, and when taken young, the most docile and susceptible of kind usage. As to the other kinds, their nature is savage and ferocious, their power is dangerous, and their haunts are to be guarded against. The numbers of maimed Indians to be seen in this country exhibit a melancholy proof of their power over the human species. A Canadian last summer had his arm lacerated in a dreadful manner by one of these destructive animals; yet if a man is mounted on a good horse, he may attack one with success; nor will they always fall on a person unprovoked. They feed on berries, roots and flesh. In summer they travel about, but in winter they live in a state of inanimation in some recesses under the ground, and sustain nature by sucking their paws.

Perhaps the last, but not the least important of these early reports was provided by Sir Alexander MacKenzie, the noted explorer. In the account of his second visit to the Northwest, published in 1801, he tells of seeing, on May 13, 1795, the tracks of a "grisly bear" on the banks of the Peace River, some of which were nine inches in width. He went on to say:

The Indians entertain great apprehension of this kind of bear, and they never venture to attack it except in a party of at least three or four.

Lack Of First-Hand Information

Significantly, none of these 17th and 18th century reports of the great bears of Canada and the Northwest really represented anything more than hearsay. Each visitor or explorer obtained his information from the natives of the region, doubtless with the usual difficulties incident to a lack of being able to understand the language well. One traveler had seen tracks of the creature, while another had seen its skin, but no one of them could say that he himself had laid eyes upon one of these remarkable animals in the flesh.

Each of the reports described was either published or eventually came to light in Europe. No corresponding stories seem to have appeared prior to 1800 in the English-speaking sections of Canada or the United States and predecessor colonies; and those in England and France, so far as the public generally paid any attention to them, were accorded about as much credence as is given today to the constantly recurring reports of "Bigfoot" in northern California and in British Columbia.

V

LEWIS AND CLARK "DISCOVER" THE GRIZZLY

One of the best-known events of American history is the trek of Captains Lewis and Clark from the Mississippi to the Pacific and return in 1804-1806. Not so well-known, however, is the story of their discoveries in the field of fauna and flora, and the fact that their most notable zoological "discovery" was the grizzly bear.

Before their memorable trip, the grizzly as a species was relatively unknown to science. While an English naturalist, on the basis of rather scanty information, had undertaken to identify the grizzly in 1784 as a separate species, no one, prior to Lewis and Clark, had been able to supply anatomical detail about this mysterious beast, based upon first-hand observation.

Soon after President Thomas Jefferson consummated the Louisiana Purchase in 1803, he authorized an expedition to explore the newly acquired territory. Putting his former secretary, Captain Meriwether Lewis in charge, he gave him detailed written instructions in reference to the objectives of the journey. Among the items which he thus directed be studied along the expedition's route were:

> The animals of the country generaly, and especially those not known in the United States.... The remains and accounts of any which may be deemed rare or extinct.

Grizzlies In The Dakotas

Lewis and Clark began to hear of an animal called the "white bear" before their expedition had proceeded very far. On October 2, 1804, when they had reached what is now central South Dakota, some 1,400 miles up the winding Missouri from St. Louis, they were given their first information concerning such a creature. Their informant was a French trader named Valle who had spent the preceding winter near the Black Mountains (Hills) where, he said, there were —

> ...great quantities of goats, white bear, prairie cocks, and a species of animal which from his description must resemble a small elk, with large circular horns.

The "white bear" was a translation of the common Indian name for the grizzly, and the animal with the "large circular horns" was, of course, the Rocky Mountain sheep.

From that time forward, the expedition began to hear and see more of this unique beast we now know as the grizzly. On October 7, 1804, the expedition's journal reports that "the tracks of a large white bear" were seen. On October 20, 1804, near what is now the border between the Dakotas, they —

> ...wounded a white bear, and saw some fresh tracks of those animals which are twice as large as the track of a man.

After wintering at Fort Mandan in present day North Dakota, the expedition resumed its westward journey on April 7, 1805. On April 10th, they saw the "track of a large white bear." Two of the animals were glimpsed on April 14th, and the tracks of others were noted on April 17th, as the party continued to move up the Missouri through what is now the northwestern part of North Dakota.

Killing Their First Grizzly

It was on April 29, 1805, just after entering the Montana of today, a few miles beyond the mouth of the Yellowstone, that they experienced their first real encounter with the legendary "white bear." The expedition's journal for that date contained the following entry:

> We proceeded early with a moderate wind. Captain Lewis who was on shore with one hunter met about eight o'clock two white bears. Of the strength and ferocity of this animal, the Indians had given us dreadful accounts. They never attack him but in parties of six or eight persons, and even then are often defeated with the loss of one

or more of the party. Having no weapons but bows and arrows, and the bad guns with which the traders supply them, they are obliged to approach very near to the bear; and as no wound except through the head or heart is mortal, they frequently fall a sacrifice if they miss their aim.

He rather attacks than avoids a man, and such is the terror which he has inspired, that the Indians who go in quest of him paint themselves and perform all the superstitious rites customary when they make war on a neighboring nation.

Hitherto those we had seen did not appear desirous of encountering us, but although to a skillful rifleman the danger is very much diminished, yet the white bear is still a terrible animal. On approaching these two, both Captain Lewis and the hunter fired, and each wounded a bear. One of them made his escape. The other turned upon Captain Lewis and pursued him 70 or 80 yards, but being badly wounded he could not run so fast as to prevent him from reloading his piece, which he again aimed at him; and a third shot from the hunter brought him to the ground. He was a male not quite full grown and weighed about 300 pounds. The legs are somewhat longer than those of the black bear, and the talons and tusks much larger and stronger... Its color is a yellowish brown, the eyes small, black and piercing, the front of the fore legs near the feet is usually black, and the fur is finer, thicker and deeper than that of the black bear. Add to that, it is a more furious animal, and remarkable for the wounds it will bear without dying.

Adventures During The Month Of May

For the next two months seldom a week would pass without some encounter between members of the expedition and one of the big bears. On Sunday, May 5, 1805, the journal contained the entry:

Captain Clark and one of the hunters met this evening the largest brown bear we have seen. As they fired he did not attempt to attack, but fled with a most tremendous roar, and such was its extraordinary tenacity of life, that although he had five balls passed through his lungs and five other wounds, he swam more than half across the river to a sandbar, and survived 20 minutes. He weighed between 500 and 600 pounds, at least, and measured eight feet seven inches and a half from the nose to the extremity of the hind feet, five feet 10½ inches round the breast, three feet eleven inches round the neck, one foot eleven inches round the middle of the fore leg, and his talons, five on each foot, were 4⅜ inches in length. It differs from the common black bear in having its talons much longer and more blunt; its tail shorter, its hair of a reddish or bay brown, longer, finer and more abundant; his liver, lungs and heart much larger even in proportion to his size, his heart particularly being equal to that of a large ox; his maw ten times larger; his testicles pendant from the belly and in separate pouches four inches apart. Besides fish and flesh he feeds on roots, and every kind of wild fruit.

On Tuesday, May 14, 1805, the expedition's journal reported another dramatic encounter with what it again referred to as a brown bear as follows:

Towards evening the men in the hindmost canoes discovered a large brown bear lying in the open grounds, about 300 paces from the river. Six of them, all good hunters, immediately went to attack him, and concealing themselves by a small eminence came unperceived within 40 paces of him. Four of the hunters now fired, and each lodged a ball in his body, two of them directly through the lungs. The furious animal sprang up and ran open-mouthed upon them. As he came near, the two hunters who had reserved their fire gave him two wounds, one of which breaking his shoulder retarded his motion for a moment; but before they could reload he was so near that they were obliged to run to the river, and before they reached it he had almost overtaken them. Two jumped into the canoe; the other four separated, and concealing themselves in the willows fired as fast as each could reload. They struck him several times, but instead of weakening the monster, each shot seemed only to direct him towards the hunter, till at last he pursued two of them so closely that they threw aside their guns and pouches, and jumped down a perpendicular bank of 20 feet into the river. The bear sprang after them, and was within a few feet of the hindmost, when one of the hunters on shore shot him in the head and finally killed him. They dragged him to the shore, and found that 8 balls had passed through him in different directions. The bear was old and the meat tough, so they took the skin only, and rejoined us at camp.

Encounters During June

On Sunday, June 2, 1805, the expedition's hunters were out the greater part of the day in search of game, and brought in six elk, two buffalo, two mule-deer and a bear. As the journal reported it,

> This last animal had nearly cost us the lives of two of our hunters who were together when he attacked them; one of them narrowly escaped being caught, and the other, after running a considerable distance, concealed himself in some thick bushes; and while the bear was in quick pursuit of his hiding place, his companion came up and fortunately shot the animal through the head.

A somewhat similar attack took place the following Saturday, June 8th, near camp during the evening. As the journal reported it,

> Near the camp this evening, a white bear attacked one of the men, whose gun happening to be wet, would not go off. He instantly made towards a tree, but was so closely pursued that as he ascended the tree he struck the bear with his foot. The bear not being able to climb, waited till he should be forced to come down; and as the rest of the party were separated from him by a perpendicular cliff of rocks, which they could not descend, it was not in their power to give him any assistance. Fortunately, however, at last the bear became affrighted at their cries and firing and released the man.

An even narrower escape was that of Captain Lewis himself on the following Friday, June 14th, while engaged in shooting one of a large herd of buffalos to provide meat for the party. According to the journal —

> The animal immediately began to bleed, and Captain Lewis who had forgotten to reload his rifle, was intently watching to see him fall, when he beheld a large brown bear stealing on him unperceived, and was already within 20 steps. In the first moment of surprise he lifted his rifle, but remembering instantly that it was not charged, and that he had not time to reload, he felt that there was no safety but in flight. It was in the open level plain, not a bush or a tree within 300 yards, the bank of the river sloping and not more than 3 feet high, so that there was no possible mode of concealment.
> Captain Lewis therefore thought of retreating in a quick walk as fast as the bear advanced toward the nearest tree; but as soon as he turned the bear ran openmouthed and at full speed upon him. Captain Lewis ran about 80 yards, but finding that the animal gained on him fast, it flashed on his mind that by getting into the water to such a depth that the bear would be obliged to attack him swimming,

there was still some chance of his life. He therefore turned short, plunged into the river about waist deep, and facing about presented the point of his spontoon.

The bear arrived at the water's edge within 20 feet of him, but as soon as he put himself in this position of defense, he seemed frightened, and wheeling about, retreated with as much precipitation as he had pursued. Very glad to be released from this danger, Captain Lewis returned to the shore, and observed him run with great speed, sometimes looking back as if he expected to be pursued, till he reached the woods. He could not conceive the cause of the sudden alarm of the bear, but congratulated himself on his escape when he saw his own track torn to pieces by the furious animal, and learned from the whole adventure never to suffer his rifle to be a moment unloaded.

Only six days later, which was Thursday, the 20th of June, Captain Clark had killed a beaver, an elk and eight buffalo, after which he sent one of the men a short distance from the camp to bring home some of the meat. As the man was on this mission, he —

...was attacked by a white bear, and closely pursued within 40 paces of the camp, and narrowly escaped being caught. Captain Clark immediately went with three men in quest of the bear which he was afraid might surprise another of the hunters who was out collecting the game. The bear, however, was too quick, for before Captain Clark could reach the man, the bear had attacked him and compelled him to take refuge in the water. He ran off as they approached, and it being late they deferred pursuing him till the next morning.

Bear Infestation Of The Camp

Efforts to locate the troublesome bear on the 21st proved fruitless, and the party remained free from bear assaults until the following Thursday, June 27th. As set forth by the expedition's journal for that date,

...the hunters came in from about four miles above us. They had killed nine elk, and three bear. As they were hunting on the river they saw a low ground covered with brushwood, where from the tracks along shore they thought a bear had probably taken refuge. They therefore landed, without making a noise, and climbed a tree about

20 feet above the ground. Having fixed themselves securely, they raised a loud shout, and a bear instantly rushed towards them. These animals never climb, and therefore when he came to the tree, Drewyer shot him in the head. He proved to be the largest we have yet seen, his nose appeared to be like that of a common ox, his fore feet measured nine inches across, and his hind feet were seven inches wide, and 11¾ inches long, exclusive of the talons. One of these animals came within 30 yards of the camp last night, and carried off some buffalo meat which we had placed on a pole.

The expedition's journal for June 28th complains of the problems being caused by bear depredations, saying:

The white bear have now become exceedingly troublesome. They constantly infest our camp during the night, and although they have not attacked us, as our dog who patrols all night gives us notice of their approach, yet we are obliged to sleep with our arms by our sides for fear of accident, and we cannot send one man alone to any distance, particularly if he has to pass through brushwood. We saw two of them today on the large island opposite to us, but as we are all much occupied now, we mean to reserve ourselves for some leisure moment, and then make a party to drive them from the islands.

Between their many duties in camp, and a stretch of bad weather, they did not get to make their assault on the island until July 2nd. They found that the part of the island frequented by the bears was covered by an almost impenetrable thicket of broad-leafed willow. The journal says:

Into this we forced our way in parties of three, but could see only one bear, who instantly attacked Drewyer. Fortunately as he was rushing on, the hunter shot him through the heart within twenty paces and he fell, which enabled Drewyer to get out of his way. We then followed him one hundred yards and found that the wound had been mortal..

West Of The Continental Divide

Lewis and Clark reached the headwaters of the Missouri on August 12, 1805 and crossed the continental divide on that same date. They arrived at the mouth of the Columbia early in November and remained on or near the Pacific shore until they commenced their homeward journey in April, 1806. While west of the Rockies, they had no problems with belligerent grizzlies, although they did shoot a few of them before re-crossing the divide in the latter part of June.

While passing through the Idaho of today, they tarried with a village of Chopunnish Indians. There they found that this tribe, which we today know as the Nez Perce, used the term "hohhost" to describe the bear now known as "grizzly," while they referred to the common black bear by the name "yackah." They showed these Indians the pelts of the various bears which they had killed nearby, as well as a very nearly white one which they had purchased. The expedition journal described the tribal comments as follows:

> The natives immediately classed the white, the deep and the pale grizzly red, the grizzly dark brown — in short, all those with the extremities of the hair of a white or frosty color, without regard to the color of the ground of the poil (pelt) under the name of hohhost. They assured us that they were all of the same species with the white bear; that they associated together, had longer nails than the others, and never climbed trees.... This distinction of the Indians seems to be well founded, and we are inclined to believe that the white, grizzly, etc. bear of this neighborhood forms a distinct species which, moreover, is the same with that of the same color on the upper part of the Missouri.

Return Via Yellowstone River

Back in Montana, the expedition, strangely enough, encountered relatively few grizzlies. One incident did occur on July 15, 1806, reported by the journal as follows:

> At night M'Neal, who had been sent in the morning to examine the cache at the lower end of the portage, returned; but had been prevented from reaching that place by a singular adventure. Just as he arrived near Willow Run, he approached a thicket of brush in which was a white bear, which he did not discover till he was within ten feet of him. His horse started, and wheeling suddenly round, threw M'Neal almost immediately under the bear, which started up instantly. Finding the bear raising himself on his hind feet to attack him, he struck him on the head with the butt end of his musket. The blow

38

was so violent that it broke the breach (sic) of the musket and knocked the bear to the ground. Before he recovered, M'Neal, seeing a willow tree close by, sprang up, and there remained while the bear closely guarded the foot of the tree until late in the afternoon. He then went off; M'Neal being released came down, and having found his horse, which had strayed off to the distance of two miles, returned to camp. These animals are, indeed, of a most extraordinary ferocity, and it is matter of wonder that in all our encounters we have had the good fortune to escape.

During the return trip, a party led by Captain Clark detoured from the outgoing route to return by way of the Yellowstone River, ultimately reuniting with the main party on the Missouri. Their only bear adventure occurred on August 2, 1806, as to which the journal reported:

The bears, which gave us so much trouble on the head of the Missouri, are equally fierce in this quarter. This morning one of them, which was on a sand-bar as the boat passed, raised himself on his hind feet; and after looking at the party, plunged in and swam toward them. He was received with three balls to the body; he then turned round and made for the shore. Toward evening, another entered the water to swim across. Captain Clark ordered the boat toward the shore, and just as the bear landed, shot the animal in the head. It proved to be the largest female they had ever seen, so old that its tusks were worn quite smooth.

Accomplishments Of The Expedition

The expedition under the command of Captains Lewis and Clark has been called the American Odyssey; without question it was one of the great explorations of all time. Its success was due to careful planning in the way of diligent collection of military and geographical intelligence, detailed logistics, and a critical selection of personnel, together with brilliant leadership by its two captains, both of them experienced Army officers.

The Expedition crossed the continent from the Mississippi to the Oregon-Washington coast, traveling in boats, on horses, and on foot a total of 7689 miles between May, 1804 and September, 1806. Their personnel included, beside the two captains, 27 white men, one negro, one Indian woman, Sacajawea, and her half-breed husband, 32 souls in all.

The expedition brought back the first maps of the Missouri/Rocky Mountain/Columbia River country, together with important linguistic, botanical, zoological, geographical and commercial collections and reports. It opened the way for a huge and profitable fur trade, and ultimately for the Americanization of the West. Most amazing of all, it carried a baby, the child of Sacajawea, with it from what is now North Dakota to the Pacific Coast and safely back.

The journals of this daring enterprise through *terra incognita* were equally remarkable, and contain a wealth of information about the country covered. A zoological reading of the text reveals, for example, that 122 species or subspecies of animals were discovered, 65 of them west of the continental divide, and 57 east of it. Chapter 24 of the text lists 25 mammals seen enroute commencing with the "brown, white or grisly bear."

Landmark In Knowledge Of The Grizzly

It is clear from any reading of the Expedition journals that the grizzly played a prominent role in the westward trek. Members of the party had looked forward to contact with the "white bear" during their months in the Dakotas. When they finally killed their firstspecimen, just after crossing into what is now Montana, it was a red letter day for all concerned. They were at some pains to place a detailed description of it in their journal.

From that time until headwaters of the Missouri were reached, grizzlies kept the party in a state of constant excitement. Whenever its members caught sight of a "white bear," they moved to attack, usually in a group of two to six men, since they found that one or two bullets from their flintlock rifles, however well directed, did not stop the animal's charge; and as often as not, the beast would charge rather than flee. The grizzly was the one truly dangerous creature encountered by the expedition and the story of their 1805 trip through the future Montana reads like the "Perils of Pauline" — a thriller every week. Only by good fortune were some members of the party able to escape with their lives, and Captain Lewis himself had more than one brush with death.

The Lewis and Clark Expedition constituted a landmark in our acquisition of knowledge about this monarch of the wilderness. Prior knowledge of such a creature had been scant and sketchy, and the Lewis and Clark experience brought the species vividly to the world's attention. In the same sense, therefore, that Columbus discovered America, the two great captains "discovered" the grizzly.

Betsy Graff

A mother grizzly with cub is always dangerous.

Ptarmigan Lake with Mts. Gould, Grinnell and Wilbur in the background.

VI

HOW THE GRIZZLY GOT ITS NAMES

Despite general interest in, and great curiosity about our big bears, the public really knows little about the grizzly. For the average citizen, the name conjures up a mental picture of a huge and dangerous beast. Beyond that, however, his information is vague, and he is understandably unaware of the origin or meaning of the word "grizzly," or how it came to be applied to this extraordinary creature.

The grizzly bear was not known by that name to oldtime Indians. The Nez Perce tribe of Idaho called it "hohhost" (whatever that meant), while other tribes had words in their language that translated to "white bear" or "grey bear." Some tribes looked upon the grizzly as a semi-divinity or ancestor, and called him their "older brother," "old man" "the big hairy one," etc.

Over the years, their white successors have applied a variety of names to the species, a fact which is not too surprising in view of the tremendous continental area over which the animals once roamed. The names "grizzly" and "grisly" have been more commonly applied; but additionally, at times, such terms as "white bear," "gray bear," "big brown bear," "silvertip," and even "golden bear" (in California) have been used — all on the basis of the coloring of the animal's pelt. In rare instances the term "roachback" has been used, Webster saying that this means "arched back," while now and then it was referred to as "baldface." Despite these differences in terminology, "grizzly" is now universally recognized as the common name for all varieties except the big brown bears of Alaska and Arctic Canada.

Special Nomenclature

The grizzly has also come to be known, with something akin to affection and admiration, by various pet names. Among these nicknames were "Old Ephraim" and "Moccasin Joe" — the former in allusion to the flatfooted way in which the bear walks, like a man, and the latter in reference to its queer, half-human footprints that look as though made by some misshapen giant, walking in moccasins. Individual grizzlies were sometimes given local cognomens, such as "Old Mose," "Nick Carter," "Grouchy," "Grandpa" and "Old Timberline."

Still another name connected with grizzly nomenclature, although in a purely peripheral way, was the teddybear, a cuddly toy that dates from the era of Theodore Roosevelt. The originator of this child's plaything took advantage of the Roosevelt popularity (he was commonly referred to as "Teddy"), and his renown as a hunter of, and writer about, the grizzly. Many an oldster of later years can still recall a "Teddy" as his or her most cherished possession, serving in some cases as a virtual security blanket.

Evolution Of The Name

The word "grizzly" crept into the language through the journals and reports of early travelers to the great Northwest. Webster provides a few clues in this direction, indicating that "grizzle" is from the Middle English word "grisel" and the French "gris," both meaning gray or grayish. "Grisly" is from the Old English "grislic," meaning horrible. Since all of the early explorers of the country west of Hudson Bay were either English or French, it was natural that they should delve into their native tongues to find appropriate adjectives. The first, of course, described the animal's appearance, while the second referred to its disposition.

It would appear to have been Samuel Hearne, the English traveler, who first used the term "grizzled" in reference to the great bears described in the report of his 1769-1772 journey to North America. He wrote of seeing the skin of an enormous "grizzled" bear, and of seeing "Grizzled Bear Hill," an area frequented by the beasts. The fact that the hill had such a name when he first viewed it suggests that those living there had already applied that name to the animal as well as the area.

Another early traveler, Edward Umfreville, used the term "grizzle bear" in 1790, while the English explorer, Sir Alexander MacKenzie, wrote of the "grisly bear" in 1801. But the first naturalist to designate the huge American bears as a separate species and to use the term "grizzly bear" seems to have been the Englishman, Thomas Pennant, in the year 1784.

Use Of The Term "Grisly"

The extent to which Lewis and Clark may have been aware of any of these terms when they undertook their tremendous safari across western America is uncertain. Their journal shows a uniform reference to the great bears which they encountered as the "white bear" or the "brown bear" until the final year of the expedition when they began to use such adjectives as "grizzly," "grisly," and "variegated," all with obvious reference to the color of the animals. As a matter of fact, it was not until the journal entry of May 31, 1806 that the word "grizzly" was used, this being in the following context:

> The natives immediately classified the white, the deep and the pale grizzly red, the grizzly dark brown — in short, all those with the extremities of the hair of a white or frosty color, without regard to the color of the ground of the poil (pelt) under the name of hohhost... This distinction of the Indians seems to be well founded, and we are inclined to believe, first, that the white or grizzly bear of this neighborhood form a distinct species, which moreover is the same with those of the same color on the upper part of the Missouri...

Only a few days earlier, on May 14, 1806, the journal had used the term "grisly," rather than "grizzly," as follows:

> The hunters killed some pheasants, two squirrels, and a male and a female bear, the first of which was large and fat, and of a bay colour; the second meagre, grisly, and of smaller size. They were of the species common to the upper part of the Missouri, and might well be termed the variegated bear, for they are found occasionally of a black, grisly brown or red colour.

This spelling, i.e., "grisly," had also appeared somewhat earlier

(Chapter 24 of the Journal) in a summary of the species of "Wild Animals" encountered by the expedition, when the phrase "the brown, white, or grisly bear" was used twice. Viewing all of these references in context, it is obvious that, regardless of the spelling (and neither of the two captains was noted for his spelling ability), the intent was to refer to the color of the animal's fur. Nowhere else in the journal is there anything to suggest that use of the word "grisly" was, in fact, meant to describe the animal's disposition.

Clinton and Brackenridge

The Lewis and Clark journal was not published until 1814, although they had returned from the West in 1806. In the interim, however, a few interested scholars apparently had access to its contents, one of whom was De Witt Clinton, distinguished statesman, scholar and naturalist. The year 1814 also saw the publication of another source of information concerning the bears of the Northwest, by H.M. Brackenridge. It was entitled "Views of Louisiana; together with a Journal of a Voyage Up the Missouri River, in 1811."

It was on May 4, 1814 (but prior to publication of the Lewis and Clark journal later that year) that De Witt Clinton presented his *Introductory Discourse* to the Literary and Philosophical Society of New York. In this notable speech, Clinton gathered together all the earlier loose ends of information concerning the "grissly bear" (as he referred to it), including data from the Lewis and Clark journal, and undertook to give them scientific significance. So complete and authentic was his discourse that it fell but little short of establishing a classification in permanent nomenclature.

Ursus horribilis

The year 1815 was an important one in the annals of the grizzly bear, for it brought onto the scene a naturalist named George Ord. It was in the second American edition of Guthrie's *Geography*, published that year, that Ord formulated a description of the species, and established three varieties of bears under *Genus Ursus: the Polar Bear (Ursus maritimus)*; the American (Black) Bear *Ursus americanus)*; and the Grizzly Bear *(Ursus horribilis)*. The accepted classifications in present-day nomenclature for the first two of these have been changed, but the popular name of "grizzly bear," given officially to this animal by Ord, has become universally accepted.

Why did Ord choose *Ursus horribilis* (from the Latin, meaning "horrible bear") as a scientific name? It would not appear to have been from the occasional spelling by Lewis and Clark of "grisly," since the word was obviously used only with reference to the color of some of the animals. Rather it would seem to have been based upon the descriptions of the grizzly's ferocity and aggressiveness, reported by both Lewis and Clark and Brackenridge. It was from the latter's book (at page 55) that Ord quoted the following lurid description of the fierceness of this species of bear:

> This animal is the monarch of the country which he inhabits. The African lion or the tiger of Bengal are not more terrible or fierce. He is the enemy of man and literally thirsts for human blood. So far from shunning, he seldom fails to attack and even to hunt him. The Indians make war upon these ferocious monsters with the same ceremonies as they do upon a tribe of their own species and, in the recital of their victories, the death of one of them gives the warrior greater renown than the scalp of a human enemy.

Other Names

At all events, *Ursus horribilis* came to be accepted as a basis for the later and more elaborate classifications of this genus and related forms, species and subspecies, although Ord's name was appended only to the one particular variety which he described, to wit, "the Big Plains Grizzly." As one writer has summed it up:

> George Ord established the common name of the animal and all his closely related kin as 'grizzly bear,' in recognition of its color characteristics; and he gave the Latin name of *horribilis* as a recognition of its pugnacious and aggressive nature.

During the years that followed Ord's historic action, a number of naturalists suggested other scientific names for the grizzly. Among these were *Ursus ferox* (De Witt Clinton), *Ursus candescens* (Hamilton Smith), and *Ursus cinereus* (Richard Harlan). However, by reason of the well established rule that the name first given to a new species by its scientific classifier shall be retained, none of these names gained any lasting recognition.

Cubs In Captivity

At this point we should pause briefly to note that a pair of grizzly cubs brought by Lieutenant Zebulon Pike from somewhere along the Santa Fe Trail in 1807 had been presented to Peale's Museum in Philadelphia. As they grew in size, their ferocity increased to the point where there was great apprehension that they might escape from their cage, so they were killed to prevent a possible catastrophe. There does not, however, seem to have been any reference to them by naturalists of the period; nor any indication that they provided either Ord or Clinton with data for their historical actions with respect to classification of the species.

About the time that Ord had formally described and named the species, there began to be an increase in western exploration and some of the travelers began to report their experiences with the grizzly. In 1823, a naturalist named T. Say, who accompanied an expedition to the Rocky Mountains under command of Major Stephen T. Long, gave a detailed scientific description and measurements of a half-grown grizzly shot by the party. In 1829, Richardson's "Fauna Boreali Americani" mentioned the fact that a grizzly cub had been captured in the Rocky Mountains, brought to England by the Hudson's Bay Company, and lodged in the London Tower. Several engravings of it were made by Edwin Landseer.

Comments By Famous People

In 1846, John J. Audubon, in his *The Viviparous Quadrupeds of North America,* set forth much information concerning the grizzly, one of which he had assisted in killing in August, 1843 on the Upper Missouri. At about this same time, Father Pierre De Smet was making his celebrated trek through the Rockies of the Northwest, encountering many species of wildlife. It was early in September, 1845 when he met his first grizzly and reported the incident thus:

> A monstrous animal, the grey bear, which replaces on our mountains the African lion, is not content with growling and menacing the intrepid venturer, who dares infringe on his cavernous dominions,

48

but grinds his teeth, expressive of his rage. Suddenly, a well-aimed gun-shot forces him to make a lowly reference; the formidable beast rolls in the dust, biting the sand saturated with his blood, and expires.

Theodore Roosevelt, foremost authority of his time on North American game animals, had engaged in ranching in the Bad Lands of western Dakota in the 1880's while grizzlies still frequented the area. He wrote extensively about the great bears, including an 1893 volume entitled *Hunting The Grisly and Other Sketches*. He preferred to refer to the species as "grisly" on the premise that

> ...the name of the bear has reference to its character, and not its color...in the same sense as horrible, exactly as we speak of a "grisly spectre," and not *grizzly*; but perhaps the latter spelling is too well established to be now changed.

While this represented his personal feeling or preference, it suggests that he was not entirely familiar with how the grizzly got its popular name.

Classification Of The Species

During the century following the return of Lewis and Clark, the grizzly was relentlessly hunted throughout the West; and dozens of specimens were collected from localities as diverse as New Mexico and Alaska. In 1918, a list of some 86 varieties of grizzlies and big brown bears was compiled by Dr. C. Hart Merriam, of the U.S. Biological Survey and Smithsonian Institution. His classifications, each accorded a name, were made to a large extent upon the basis of a study of the extensive collection of skulls in the National Museum. In many cases, no other information was available.

Other naturalists during and subsequent to Merriam's day have used various names for the grizzlies of Glacier Park. Vernon Bailey, also writing in 1918, used the term *Ursus horribilis imperator*. R.R. Lechleitner, in the 1969 edition of his book entitled *Mammals of Glacier National Park*, referred to the big bears as *Ursus arctos horribilis*. Authorities now seem to agree that all grizzly and brown bears really constitute one species to be known as *Ursus arctos*, and that local groups or so-called subspecies should be referred to merely as "populations."

49

This nomenclature has been adopted by Glacier's official Research Biologist, Clifford J. Martinka, who comments that it is now generally recognized as appropriate. He refers to the grizzlies of Glacier National Park in his various published treatises about them as *Ursus arctos,* and it would appear that the term *Ursus horribilis* can no longer be officially applied to the grizzlies of the Park or, for that matter, to any member of the species.

Mike Sample

Grizzly feeding on an elk carcass, most likely that of an old animal that failed to survive the winter.

VII

GRIZZLY MYTHS

Intimacy with a grizzly is a relationship rarely achieved, even between one grizzly and another. Old Ephraim is simply not a sociable creature. The animal's lack of approachability has tended to envelope it with an aura of mystery and to give it, to some extent, an almost legendary status. Many long-held beliefs about its habits and characteristics have turned out to be exaggerated or without foundation. Even today, grizzly lore is composed of a combination of fact and supposition.

Some of the stories about the grizzly are almost akin to superstition. One of the earliest and strangest bits of misbelief was that the bears "suck their paws" as a means of subsistence during their long winter sleeps. This myth appears as far back as 1791 when Edward Umfreville, in telling about the bears west of Hudson's Bay, stated:

> In summer they travel about, but in winter they live in a state of inanimation in some recesses under the ground, and sustain nature by sucking their paws.

Father DeSmet Repeats The Myth

This venerable bit of folklore is rather frequently encountered. Father Pierre DeSmet, in his book entitled *Oregon Missions and Travels Over the Rocky Mountains in 1845-46,* described the autumnal spawning of salmon at the headwaters of the Columbia River, attended by crowds of "grey and black bear, the wolf, the eagle and the vulture." He went on to say:

> From thence, when the snow begins to fall, the bears plump and fat, resume the road back to their dens in the thick of the forests, and hollows of rocks, there to pass the four sad wintry months in complete indolence, with no other pastime or occupation, than that of sucking their four paws. If we may credit the Indians, each paw occupies the bear for one moon (a month) and the task accomplished, he turns on the other side, and begins to suck the second, and so on with the rest.

Both Umfreville and DeSmet obtained their information from the Indians, and one can only suppose that it grew out of their wonder at the grizzly's ability to sustain life without food or water over a period of many months. Since no one dared to intrude upon the privacy of the hibernal den, the myth about the sucking of paws represented an attempt to find an explanation for the seemingly unexplainable. Doubtless, it had originated in antiquity, and was handed down from generation to generation of natives until, ultimately, it had spread to every tribe throughout the length and breadth of the Northwest.

A Solitary Beast

The grizzly is not, as many have supposed, a gregarious animal. Sometimes a number of bears may assemble together, in what looks like a group, at some favorite feeding ground — usually where the berries are thick, or by the banks of a salmon-thronged stream — but the association is never more than momentary, each going his own way as soon as hunger has been satisfied. An exception to the general pattern occurs during the rutting season, when the males seek the opposite sex. Then two or three may come together in the course of their pursuit and rough courtship of the females; and if the rivals are well-matched, savage battles follow, so that many of the old males have their heads seamed with scars made by their fellows' teeth.

The only grizzlies that ordinarily move about in a group are a sow and her cubs, and such families may travel together for a second and sometimes even a third summer. A mother bear views the meandering boar with suspicion. If convinced that he threatens her cubs, she charges him without hesitation, and the same is true of other animals, including man, which she may encounter. A pecking order usually develops among the grizzlies of a region, based upon aggressiveness. Sows with cubs are more aggressive than the barren ones, and defer only to the large males.

Another erroneous idea is that black and grizzly bears occasionally interbreed. The range of color in both species from cinnamon through brown and black has apparently given rise to a supposition that some, at least, of the bears of the Rocky Mountain region have been the result of cross breeding.

Nothing could be farther from the truth. Those who were spectators in the days when bears fed at the garbage dumps of the great hotels in Yellowstone and Glacier will recall the celerity with which a black bear would slip away whenever a grizzly appeared on the scene. And anyone who has noted the agility with which a black bear will take to a tree if a grizzly happens along will not need the opinion of science to help him discredit this bit of genealogical speculation.

Other Misbeliefs

One of the most widely disseminated myths about grizzlies is that they will rise to their full heights and leave their marks upon trees as a kind of challenge to would-be-rivals. It has been asserted that these are purposely made and duly heeded as a sort of "warning against trespassers" to mark the limits of the range claimed by the bear making them. On this theory, the bear with the tallest mark would be the "boss" of the ward. Supposedly, an ambitious young grizzly in search of a territory of its own will wander from one locale to another, checking the various marks until it finds one it can top by an inch or two.

There is at least a grain of truth in these tales, for grizzlies do occasionally rise to their full heights and bite chunks out of trees. There has, however, been no authentic explanation for such a practice. It may well be some intuitive ursine reaction similar to a cat's flexing of claws against a tree or piece of furniture, or a dog's instinctive reaction to a fireplug or tree. Bear experts who have watched grizzlies go through such a performance are convinced that it is quite without hidden significance.

The idea that a grizzly deliberately stands up and walks toward his antagonist like one of the principals in a prize ring is a mistaken one. A grizzly will, upon any pretext, stand up and look about him. Whenever he sees, or thinks he may be going to see anything, he rises to his full height on his hind legs; but those familiar with the big bears say they have never seen one continue in this posture while charging an adversary.

Similarly, the longstanding belief that bears hug their victims to death is pure fiction. The men who have lived through a "hand-to-hand" fight with an enraged grizzly probably would have preferred such bloodless tactics. At all events, there is no truth in the idea beyond the fact that a grizzly, in attacking a large animal such as a steer, will sometimes hold it with one paw while he strikes it or rips it open with the other.

Tenacity of Life

The stories about the extraordinary vitality of the grizzly are legend, and had their genesis largely in the Lewis and Clark accounts of encounters with grizzlies of the upper Missouri. However, much of the subsequent literature on the subject also bristled with statements in regard to the grizzly's tenacity of life, his ability to disregard awful wounds, and the amount of lead which he was able to absorb and still survive.

Lewis and Clark hardly ever mentioned killing one of these animals without dwelling on the ability of the species to take punishment, and it is made evident that this, as much as any other fact, contributed to the awe with which they regarded them. According to the expedition journal, the bear encountered on May 14, 1805 absorbed a total of eight "balls" before it finally succumbed. The one killed on May 5 1805 was the largest they had seen up to that date and

> ...such was its extraordinary tenacity of life that, although he had five balls passed through his lungs and five other wounds, he swam more than half across the river to a sandbar and survived twenty minutes.

In summing up the feeling of members of the expedition, the

journal commented:

> The wonderful power of life which these animals possess renders them dreadful, their very track in the mud or sand...is alarming, and we would rather encounter two Indians than meet a single brown (meaning grizzly) bear.

An Expert Speaks

A study of this subject made in some depth by one of the great authorities on the grizzly, William H. Wright, has led him to a number of conclusions. To begin with, he believes that it is only human nature (especially when badly armed) to be more impressed with the vitality of the animal which, when wounded, takes the offensive, than with the vitality of one that, when similarly wounded, invariably runs away. He says:

> Of course, the question of armament is not one to be lost sight of in reviewing the testimony of the early hunters. Their rifles were mostly smooth-bores of small calibre, not larger than the present .32, carrying bullets in many cases seventy to the pound, and all of them were muzzle-loaders with no definite charges of powder. Their penetration, variable under such circumstances, was always slight as compared with the present perfected weapons, and it was impossible for them to drive a ball through the shoulders of a tough old grizzly or even of a young one.
>
> Armed with such a weapon it was necessary to approach very near to one's quarry, the chances of killing a large animal with one shot were small, and it took time to reload. *And the wounded grizzly was a fighter.*
>
> Now it really is not at all distinctive of the grizzly that one attacked with weapons of small range and penetration should, even though having five balls in the lungs and other wounds, swim half-way across a river and survive twenty minutes; or that one shot once through the lungs should go a mile, lie up in the woods, and be found 'still perfectly alive' an hour later. Every hunter of elks or goats could match these instances with others at least equally remarkable. *But these animals run away.*
>
> If one thinks to lose one's life by an ineffectual shot, the refusal of the animal to drop at the first fire is far more impressive than if one thinks only to lose a deer. The difference is psychological, and lies

55

not in the comparative vitalities of the wounded animals, but in the varying effects of this vitality on the man behind the gun.

Voice Of Experience

Wright was speaking as a man who had more than 50 years of experience hunting the grizzly with rifles and camera. He emphasized the fact that a great deal of the animal's ability to survive one or more bullets was largely dependent upon the location of the wound, and that unless the bullet struck a lethal area of the brain or heart, the bear might well survive, or at least make good its escape. He concluded that the legendary tenacity of the grizzly to life was largely a myth, saying:

> ...I have killed well over a hundred grizzlies without finding them any more tenacious of life than many other wild animals. They cannot stand any more punishment than the deer or the elk, and they cannot begin to stand up under the rain of bullets that an old Rocky Mountain goat will survive.

VIII

GRIZZLIES: AGGRESSIVE OR DEFENSIVE?

Perhaps the most ancient and enduring belief about the grizzly has had to do with its ferocity and aggressiveness. Long antedating the coming of the white man, it became deeply rooted in the folklore and legends of tribes of the Northwest. The grizzly was the one beast that struck terror, as well as awe, into the heart of every Indian; and with good reason, for the grizzly bear, pursued into its fastnesses and attacked with bows and arrows, could be a terrible creature indeed.

The early explorers were warned by the Indians that the grizzly was a ferocious beast. They accepted the Indian verdict and thought it upheld by their own experiences. For many of them, their only knowledge of the animal was hearsay information passed along by natives. When they came to face the big bears on a hostile basis, armed only with the muzzle-loading smooth-bores of small calibre and still smaller penetration, they found antagonists almost as formidable as they had seemed to the bow and arrow wielders.

Of course, the grizzly had, and still has, a great deal going for him. He is an animal that might well be put at the head of the earth's wild life, since he has brain as well as brawn. He is self-contained and prepared for anything. In addition to an impressive appearance, he has bulk, agility, strength, poise, courage and a tremendous curiosity. He is a masterful fighter if forced to defend himself.

Before the days of the repeating rifle, the grizzly wandered boldly over his domain, master of all he surveyed. From the time the first reports of the great bears of North America began to reach Europe, their very name became synonymous with ferocity and aggressiveness, a distinction that continued to grow with reports of every returning traveler. It was reinforced by the Lewis and Clark experience; and Naturalist Ord, by tagging the grizzly with the scientific or Latin name of *horribilis,* made a major contribution to its reputation for bloodthirstiness and hostility toward man.

As the West underwent exploration, many of its colorful heroes had adventures with the grizzly, some of them literally hair-raising. Among those who lived to tell the tale after such an encounter were Kit Carson, Joe Meek, Hugh Glass and Malcolm Clark. Father De-Smet added his fuel to the flames, and even Theodore Roosevelt stressed the "grisly" character of the great bears. No wonder that the average citizen's impression of the grizzly as a most formidable and dangerous beast became indelibly fixed in the 19th century.

Questions Raised

As time went on, naturalists and others began to question the validity of early beliefs concerning the grizzly's ferocity, and to seek a dispassionate conclusion on the subject. To be weighed, on the one hand, were sincere convictions and repeated statements of early writers, together with a century of unquestioning belief on the part of the public. To be considered, on the other hand, were calmer judgments of trained observers, and the overwhelming weight of contemporaneous experience. Were early observers of the grizzly wrong about its nature? Or had the animal radically changed in a hundred years?

Eventually the evidence in support of the grizzly grew in volume and came from many knowledgable individuals. It began to be noted, moreover, that the majority of those who held the opinion that he was not ferocious were the same people who had studied him without attempting to kill him; while the majority of those saying that he was ferocious were people who had killed or had gone forth with the intention of killing him.

John Muir, eminent wilderness philosopher, in his book entitled *Steep Trails,* said:

> There are bears in the woods, but not in such numbers nor of such unspeakable ferocity as town-dwellers imagine, nor do bears spend

their lives in going about the country like the devil, seeking whom they may devour. Oregon bears, like most others, have no liking for man, either as meat or as society; and while some may be curious at times to see what manner of creature he is, most of them have learned to shun people as deadly enemies.

Dr. W. T. Hornaday (first director of the New York Zoological Garden) offered a similar opinion in his book on *The American Natural History*:

> I have made many observations on the temper of the Grizzly Bear, and am convinced that naturally the disposition of this reputedly savage creature is rather peaceful and good-natured. At the same time, however, no animal is more prompt to resent an affront or injury, or punish an offender. The Grizzly temper is defensive, not aggressive; and unless the animal is cornered, or *thinks he is cornered*, he always flees from man.

Comulative Evidence

Drummond, an early botanist, had numerous experiences with grizzlies in the Rocky Mountains in 1826. He was familiar with their curiosity, and said that often they came close and stood up to look at him. But if he made a noise with his specimen-box, or even waved his hand, they ran away.

James Capen Adams, noted California hunter and trapper of the middle 19th century, was a man who had captured many grizzlies, both old and young, and had literally tamed them. He knew them intimately, and in summing up after years of close association, said of the grizzly, "He did not invite combat."

One of the greatest experts on the grizzly was William H. Wright, who spent most of his time over a period of fifty years as a hunter of the big bears with gun and camera. He first studied them in order to hunt them successfully; then laid aside his rifle and hunted them in order to study and photograph them. As Wright points out, elaborate arguments have been presented in support of the theory that contact with man has changed the grizzly from a savage and aggressive brute to a wary and cautious animal. But he adheres to the view that the notion that the grizzly ever roamed about seeking for whomsoever he might devour is sheer nonsense, and that he will ordinarily attack on sight is a myth.

Wright made a special study of the Lewis and Clark journal with reference to its record of grizzly encounters. He noted that its authors, in writing of their early contacts with the grizzly had overlooked two salient features of their experiences: (1) that they were themselves invariably the attacking party; and (2) that even so, for every bear that stayed to fight them, there were one or more that ran away. And he felt that there was really very little that he would have expected to have been different a century later, given similar circumstances and similar weapons. Possibly fewer of the bears would show fight, since contact with man has merely added to the grizzly's caution. This, however, is not to say that today's grizzly, if cornered, would not become exceedingly dangerous.

Reinterpreting The Evidence

As a part of his analysis of their journal, Wright cited the Lewis and Clark complaint about the bears that had "infested their camp at night" while they were on the upper Missouri, and their attributing immunity from harm to themselves as being due only to the watchfulness of the camp dog. Scoffing at this, Wright suggests that if the bears had really been bent on human slaughter, the dog would have been but an appetizer for their feast. He then mentions a number of similar nocturnal visits from his own experience. Incidentally, other similar episodes in the Glacier Park area are described herein at page 14 of Chapter 1, involving Hidden Lake, and at pages 91-93 of Chapter 11, involving the Cut Bank Valley. He points out that a cardinal trait of the grizzly is its great curiosity, often causing it to investigate trails and camps, but without intent to harm the occupants.

Wright also undertook to review the incident from the Lewis and Clark journal of June 14, 1805 wherein a grizzly unexpectedly came upon Captain Lewis when his rifle was not loaded and, after pursuing him so long as he ran away, fled itself as soon as Lewis "faced round on it." With respect to this episode, puzzling to the writer of the journal, Wright felt that if properly interpreted, the incident would throw a different light on the grizzly's supposed ferocity, and one not too surprising to a person with more intimate knowledge of the species. Said Wright:

Certainly a braver man than Captain Meriwether Lewis never faced a bear, and this fact (knowing what we know) adds an element of humor to the scene. On that day, it will be recalled, Captain Lewis had shot a young buffalo, and, without having recharged his muzzle-loader, was waiting for the animal to bleed to death.

Suddenly he beheld a large brown bear which was stealing on him unperceived and was already within twenty paces. Remember, please, what the captain had been told about this animal; remember how long it took to reload the gun he carried; look again at the photograph of a curious grizzly 'stealing up unperceived,' and imagine his state of mind!

He was on an 'open, level plain — not a bush or tree within three hundred yards.' The river bank was low and offered no concealment. There was hope only in flight, and not much hope in that. In this dilemma the captain 'thought of retreating at a quick walk as fast as the bear advanced, but as soon as he turned the bear ran open-mouthed and at full speed upon him.'

Now Captain Lewis was a brave man and likewise a truthful one. We do not for an instant question his complete sincerity. But, in view of the sequel, we may, perhaps, query the 'open-mouthed' and question the 'full speed.' For, starting with a lead of twenty paces, Captain Lewis was still twenty feet ahead at the end of the race, and an 'open-mouthed bear at full speed' would have had him in six jumps. Be that as it may, however, the captain, when he had run eighty yards, finding that the bear was gaining, bethought him that he might stand a better show if the bear had to attack him swimming.

'He therefore turned short, plunged into the water, and facing about, presented the point of his espontoon. The bear arrived at the water's edge within twenty feet of him, but as soon as he put himself in this posture of defense the bear seemed frightened and, wheeling about, retreated with as much precipitation as he had pursued. Captain Lewis returned to the shore and observed him run with great speed, sometimes looking back as if he expected to be pursued, till he reached the woods.'

Now it may be thought that even a ferocious bear might be terrified by the 'presented point of an espontoon'; but never having owned one of those mysterious weapons, and having, nevertheless, seen scores of grizzlies act for all the world as this one did in its retreat, I do not believe that this terrible engine of destruction (Webster defines it as a 'half-pike') had anything to do with it. Indeed, I have no manner of doubt that if the captain had thought of his espontoon in the first instance, or if he had so much as waved a hand above the head, the encounter would have ended then and there.

Looking At It From The Bear's Viewpoint

Based upon his own fifty years of grizzly observation, Wright stated that he knew of no instance where a grizzly had turned out of its way, unprovoked, to attack a human being. He felt that in passing judgment upon bears, one must take into consideration the viewpoint of the bear. A mother with cubs that charges an intruder approaching too close to her, or a sleeping bear over which a man stumbles in a wood and which strikes him down — these must be given the benefit of their own doubts. But there are not many cases on record where people have been attacked by a grizzly in which the offender, if arraigned before a jury of his peers, could not have successfully maintained a plea of self-defense.

As Wright sums the situation up, it would seem to be beyond doubt that a century's contact with men armed with rifles has rendered the grizzly bear a more wary and cautious animal. It would, indeed, be strange if this were not so, for the grizzly is quick to learn, and has had innumerable opportunities to do so. He concludes with the comment —

> But that, during this time, the grizzly has changed from a blood-thirsty and ferocious tyrant to an inoffensive minder of his own business, 'defensive, not aggressive,' I can find nothing in the records to show, nor do I for a moment believe.

Similar testimony comes from Paul Russell Cutright who, at page 142 of his book entitled *Lewis and Clark: Pioneering Naturalists,* has the following comment:

> Unfortunately, Lewis and Clark gained most of their information about the disposition of the grizzly while looking down the barrels of their Kentucky rifles. They saw only the wounded animal maddened with pain and fear. At such times, modern big-game hunters agree, it is truly one of the most fearsome beasts on earth. But this same animal, undisturbed and unprovoked, when not cornered, wounded, or its young threatened, is far from being the dangerous creature often depicted.

A Final Circumstance To Be Considered

In any comparison of the grizzly's ferocity at the time of Lewis and Clark with that of a century later, Wright had in mind the possible changes in temperament brought about through the bears having been hunted almost to extinction over the period in question. In the national parks, with their game refuge status, there has, of course, been a complete reversal of this persecution by man — a reversal which, in the case of Glacier, has been in effect for upwards of 65 years and for many generations of bears. This freedom from persecution has been in effect for a much longer period in Yellowstone Park. Said Enos Mills in his 1919 book on *The Grizzly*:

> The experience with bears in the Yellowstone Park demonstrates that the grizzly is not ferocious. The Park had a numerous grizzly population when it was made a wild-life reservation. The people who in increasing numbers visited the Park carried no firearms and they were not molested by the grizzlies. Yet grizzlies were all about. After some twenty years of this friendly association of people and grizzlies, a number of grizzlies, dyspeptic and demoralized from eating garbage, and annoyed by the teasing of thoughtless people, became cross and lately even dangerous. Eliminate the garbage piles and cease harassing the bears, and they will again be friendly.

Glacier Park has eliminated the garbage piles and is going to great lengths to educate its visitors on how to conduct themselves with reference to bears. The Park experience seems to demonstrate that, even in an area filled with summer visitors thronging over trails and through backcountry, nearly all of the grizzlies, if not quite 100%, prefer to go quietly about their business, avoiding humans as much as possible. Certainly it rather effectively demolishes the myth of grizzlies as the ferocious, aggressive and man-hating creatures so luridly pictured by Lewis and Clark, George Ord and many others of the 19th century.

63

To Red Rock Falls with the Garden Wall in the background.

IX

GRIZZLIES AS PETS

In view of the longstanding differences as to the grizzly's ferocity or lack of it, the reader may find it hard to believe that there are many well documented cases of tamed grizzlies, adults as well as youngsters. But 19th century annals of the Old West contain many instances where members of the species, when captured as cubs and treated with kindness, became personal pets. Some of these remarkable relationships developed in California, others in Colorado and Wyoming.

Lola Montez, the celebrated California actress of goldrush days, is said to have had a pair of half-grown grizzlies which she kept chained on either side of her front porch at Grass Valley. And Bret Harte wrote a highly entertaining account of a grizzly cub's sojourn in a San Francisco boarding house. It humorously relates the reactions of a small bear to a new environment, telling of his alertness and versatility under changed and unexacting conditions. The story appears in Harte's *Tales Of The Argonauts and Other Sketches*, published in Boston in 1875 by the Regent Press.

Jim and Bessie

Then there was the case of two grizzly cubs that were brought in by a cowboy who, while hunting on a Wyoming ranch, had killed their mother. The return to the ranch house was something of an adventure, not without some loss of skin and clothing by their captor. Originally named Jim and Bessie before their gender had been ascertained, their names were soon changed, in the interests of accuracy, to Miss Jim and Mr. Bessie.

According to the ranch owner, Philip Rollins, the cubs were introduced to their sleeping quarters in the "bear parlor," an enclosure connected with the main room of the ranch house by a doorway usually closed only with several curtains of heavy felt. In that "parlor" lived five black bears, and the advent of the little grizzlies was accompanied by pandemonium and much clawing and biting. However, it didn't take long before Miss Jim and Mr. Bessie were in full control of the situation, and had become friends of all the men except one, who could not refrain from teasing them. When the teasing had continued for some months, the little grizzlies having in the meantime increased in size, strength and resentment, a visiting surgeon had to be called in to treat three ribs and a fractured arm of their tormentor.

As the young bears grew older, they were given the run of the premises, coming and going at will in and out of the ranch house. They attended ranch meals, perched on a bench at the foot of the dining-table; and, after the first six months, made any excursion they wished, being absent from the ranch at times for several successive days, either alone or with one of the men. Some of these trips were fishing parties, and on such occasions the cubs were usually content with their toll of the first four fish caught; that is, two apiece.

Good Manners

On their bench at the foot of the dining-table, they were never indecorous, but would sit in dignified silence until called by name. On hearing its name, the invited bear would shuffle to the chair of the inviter and, having been given the promised morsel, would promptly return to its seat. Special care was taken, however, that they should be fed before approaching either the dining-table in the ranch house or the lunching group of a fishing party.

During the next four years, the grizzlies demonstrated on many occasions their faithfulness, intelligence, and an endless sense of humor. No untoward incidents developed until, unexpectedly, Miss Jim fell victim to poison, whether set for her or for wolves was never learned. Soon after that, Mr. Bessie was once more teased, this time by a visiting ranchman. After the latter had been revived and reassembled, it was decided that the bear must be disposed of, though not killed. They didn't want him to be caged in a zoological garden, since he had not sinned according to bear law. It was agreed that he should be lost.

Accordingly, the grizzly was transported some two hundred miles from the ranch and bidden to go his way. His return to the ranch preceded that of his transporter by eight hours, this being in the days before automotive vehicles. He was then taken to the mountains of Idaho, and the duration of his return journey not improbably is still the record for that course. Finally, two of his admirers conducted him to Oregon and there took their leave of him. Their last view of him disclosed a cheerful expression as he contemplated two hams tied to a tree, partly for purposes of strategy and partly as a parting gift. And that was the last ever heard of Mr. Bessie.

Miss Grizzly

A female cub captured by the foreman of a sawmill located in the Medicine Bow Mountains of Wyoming soon became the pet and favorite of all the men in camp. She had the freedom of the premises, played with visiting teamsters, and welcomed strangers, although somewhat boisterously and in a way to frighten those not aware of her friendly intentions.

She was never chained and rambled about wherever she liked; however, she spent most of her time near the mill. Occasionally she followed one of the loggers off into the woods, and would lie near where he was working, interested in the flying chips. One day a falling tree sent a shower of limbs all about Miss Grizzly, as she was called, one of them apparently striking her. Although not injured, she was startled and, bawling like a frightened baby, turned and ran for camp. After that, she never again went into the woods with that logger.

She was usually fed just outside the cook-house door, and preferred to eat in seclusion. But when especially hungry, she came boldly into the dining-room where the men were eating. Walking around the table, she accepted whatever was offered her — and everyone offered her something.

She was always independent and resourceful. One day a teamster handed her a bottle of catsup. Standing erect, she took it deftly in her fore paws. She held it between her eyes and the light, seemingly interested in its color, then shook it back and forth close to her ear. Then, going to a nearby log, she brought the bottle down on it and catsup splashed in all directions. Her curiosity satisfied, she seemed to enjoy licking up the contents.

Playfulness and Excursions

While the men never attempted to teach Miss Grizzly tricks, she enjoyed cartwheeling and liked to have the men start her with a little push down the slope near the mill. Curling her nose behind her toes, she rolled over and over. Occasionally she climbed upon the flat-roofed lumber shed for the fun of rolling off. While she did much climbing over the logs and lumber piles and on the low roofs, she did not attempt to climb a tree after the first few weeks at the mill.

One day during her third summer at the mill, she followed one of the teamsters away and did not return until sometime in the night. After this she made an occasional excursion into the woods alone, sometimes being gone a day or two. One day, after an unusually long absence, she came back accompanied by another young grizzly. The latter was seemingly hesitant to approach the mill, although Miss Grizzly had apparently turned back to reassure him. Both finally came within a short distance of the mill, but at the appearance of one of the men, the stranger turned and fled.

The first winter she did not offer to hibernate and the men never thought to encourage her to den up. But the second winter she slept three months in a den which she had dug back into the side of a big sawdust pile. Two or three times during the winter the men wakened her, and she came to the mouth of the den and then returned to sleep. Once she came out for a few hours but, though tempted, refused to eat. The third autumn at the mill Miss Grizzly made numerous excursions into the woods alone, and one day she left on a trip from which she did not return.

Jenny and Johnny

Enos A. Mills, renowned as the father of Rocky Mountain National Park, was one of the great friends of the grizzly. One day in the late years of the 19th century he came upon two small grizzly cubs, each about the size of a cottontail rabbit. Knowing that their mother had been killed, he captured them after a lively chase, in which both he and his clothes were pretty well chewed up, and carried them home in a sack.

He shook them out of the sack in front of a basin of milk and thrust their noses deeply into it. After being without food for three days, they took to it readily, and had become pets before sundown. Within twenty-four hours, Jenny knew that her name was Jenny, and Johnny that his was Johnny. After a few days they followed Mills around with fondness and loyalty.

When they were small, they would come close to Mills if he were sitting down, stand on their hind legs, put their fore paws on his knees and look up at him. They would play with his watch chain, peep into his pockets, or look at the buttons on his coat. Sometimes they would climb up into his lap, twitch his ears, touch his nose, play with his hair, and finally fall off to sleep, one on each arm. They grew rapidly. At the age of seven months, Johnny weighed approximately sixty pounds, and Jenny forty-six.

Numerous visitors and the increasing size of the cubs at last made it necessary for Mills to chain them. They were almost always on the move, either pacing back and forth or circling. Their long chains often got tangled with sticks, grass or bushes. Sometimes they showed impatience, but usually they carefully examined the chain, then taking it in their fore paws, would step this way and that, generally making the very moves needed to extricate or unwind it. While doing this, they appeared almost comical because of their serious and concentrated attention.

Intolerance For Teasing

One September Mills took Jenny and Johnny camping out in Wild Basin, the two bears racing along as happy as two children. Sometimes they were ahead of him, sometimes behind; occasionally they paused to wrestle and box. At night they lay close to him beside the campfire. Often he used one of them for a pillow, and more than once he awoke to find that they were using him for one.

As they were climbing along the top of a moraine, a black bear and her two cubs came within perhaps thirty feet. The cubs and their

Hikers near Granite Park Lodge, with Heaven's Peak in the right background.

mother bristled up and ran off terribly frightened, while Johnny and Jenny only a short distance in front of Mills, walked on, ludicrously pretending that they had not seen the black bears.

The man who was in charge of Mills' place when he was away neither understood nor sympathized with wideawake and aggressive young grizzlies, and once when Mills was absent, he teased Johnny. The inevitable crash came and the man went to the hospital. On another occasion he set a pan of sour milk on the ground before Jenny. While bears learn to like sour milk, Jenny had not yet learned and she sniffed at it disdainfully. "Drink it," the man roared, and kicked her in the ribs. Again it was necessary to send for the ambulance.

At last it appeared best to send Jenny and Johnny to the Denver Zoo. Two years went by before Mills allowed himself the pleasure of visiting them. A number of other bears were with them in a large pen, when he leaped in, calling "Hello, Johnny!" Johnny jumped up, fully awake, stood erect, extended both arms, and gave a few joyful grunts in the way of greeting. Back among the other bears stood Jenny on tiptoe, eagerly looking on.

Grizzly Adams

Perhaps the most extraordinary, yet authentic, record of pet grizzlies concerns James Capen Adams, who came from Massachusetts to California, and in the fall of 1852 took up the life of a hermit, hunter and purveyor of wild animals to shows and menageries. The story of his amazing, though brief, career is told in a book called *The Adventures of James Capen Adams, Mountaineer and Grizzly Bear Hunter of California*, written by Theodore H. Hittell, well-known California historian, and published in 1860.

Grizzly Adams, as he became known, made his headquarters in the central Sierra Nevada Mountains during the years 1852-1855, but his first grizzly acquisition was a female captured in 1853, along with two unrelated white cubs, in the vicinity of what is now Glacier Park, then in the Territory of Washington, and given the name of Lady Washington. Captured as a yearling, Lady Washington, through kindness and training, became Adams' constant companion and friend.

In the spring of 1854 he captured a cub at the headwaters of the

71

Merced River, and gave it the name of Benjamin Franklin. Ben became the favorite of Adams, who described him rather quaintly as: "The most excellent of all beasts, as faithful as it is possible for any animal to be; Ben Franklin, the king of the forest, the flower of his race, my firmest friend."

When Ben became larger, Adams trained him as a pack animal, and Ben carried the camp outfit and supplies on his back through the wilderness. At other times he was used with Rambler, a greyhound, and was never chained except when near a village, and then only for the safety of the excited dogs. On one of his hunting expeditions, Adams came unexpectedly upon a mother grizzly with cubs while passing through a thicket. The mother bear with one paw knocked Adams' gun aside before he could fire, then with the other struck him and peeled the scalp down over his eyes. At that point Ben Franklin and Rambler, who were close behind him, sprang to his assistance, the dog attacking the grizzly's rear and Ben her front.

Ben Becomes A Savior

While the grizzly was thus occupied with Ben and the dog, Adams recovered his gun and shot the bear through the heart. When she began to show signs of recovery, he closed in on her with his knife and finished her off with half a dozen strokes. Back at camp, he rendered first aid to Ben, then trimmed the edges of his own scalp, washed the wounds, and applied a bandage. Both man and grizzly carried the scars of that battle to their dying days, and Adams' injuries eventually played a part in his demise a few years later.

Among all the animals collected by Adams, one of the most remarkable was Sampson, a grizzly trapped in midwinter of 1854-55 in the midst of a pine forest in the general vicinity of his central Sierra Nevada Camp. Sampson was much the largest of his grizzly group, assertedly weighing more than 1500 pounds. It was after the capture of Sampson that Adams rented space on Clay Street, near Leidesdorf, in San Francisco and established his Mountaineer Museum, advertising in September, 1856 as follows:

72

Great Show of Animals
MOUNTAINEER MUSEUM
at 142 Clay Street
LARGEST COLLECTION OF WILD ANIMALS
ever exhibited on the Pacific Coast
SAMPSON – The largest Grizzly Bear ever caught
weighing 1,510 pounds
LADY WASHINGTON – With her cub, weighing 1,000 pounds
BENJAMIN FRANKLIN – King of the Forest
Two young *WHITE BEARS FROM THE ROCKY MOUNTAINS*
ELK, LION, TIGER, PANTHER, DEER
and numberless small animals
Open from 10 A.M. to 12 P.M.
From 2 to 5 P.M. and 7 to 10 P.M.

Partner With Barnum

After two months, the menagerie was moved to the California Exchange at Clay and Kearny Street and on December 8, 1956 was reopened as the Pacific Museum. Other animals were added and the admission charge was raised to 50 cents, but the big grizzlies continued to be the main attractions. The exhibit was given a great deal of publicity in the San Francisco Daily Evening Bulletin for which Hittell was then a reporter. Ben Franklin died on January 18, 1858, and Adams eventually closed his exhibit in May, 1859, apparently for financial reasons.

He left the California scene in January, 1860, taking passage with his menagerie on the *Golden Fleece,* sailing for New York. It was about that time that Phineas T. Barnum was establishing himself as the premier showman of America. On arrival, Adams promptly got in touch with Barnum and entered into a partnership to exhibit his animals in a canvas tent at 13th and Broadway, under the name of the "California Menagerie." Barnum acted as the business manager and Adams looked after the animals. On the opening morning, a band of music preceded a procession of animal cages down Broadway and up the Bowery. This was the advent of grizzlies on New York's Broadway!

After the exhibition had been open for six weeks, Adams' doctor insisted that he should sell out his share in the animals and settle up his worldly affairs, because of the debilitating effect of his many wounds upon his health. When Adams conveyed this information to Barnum, the latter agreed to buy him out at a figure proposed by Adams. The latter made a deal, however, to continue in charge of the animals for another ten weeks for the sum of $500, and barely lasted out the agreed period.

Adams died in his former home on October 25, 1860, and is buried in the cemetery at Charlton, Massachusetts. His beloved grizzlies, along with the rest of his celebrated "California Menagerie," continued to be regular attractions at the Barnum Museum for years. While they were eventually sold, the ultimate fate of Lady Washington, Sampson and their fellow bears does not seem to have been made a matter of record for posterity.

X

HUNTING THE GRIZZLY
NEAR LAKE ST. MARY

Henry L. Stimson, later to serve as a cabinet member under three American presidents, spent a number of vacations in the region that was to become Glacier National Park. As often as he could manage it between 1891, when he first visited the St. Mary country with George Bird Grinnell, and 1913, when he finished his term as Secretary of War under President Taft, Stimson arranged to get away to Montana from his New York City law practice for a month to six weeks — usually in early autumn.

Although an easterner by birth and residence, Stimson had always craved the outdoor life. As he said in the opening paragraph of his privately printed book entitled *My Vacations,* published in 1949,

> In my early days just following the Civil War, there was still a western frontier in the United States with untamed Indians and wild animals in great numbers. I longed to see it — to hunt game, particularly dangerous game like the grizzly bear.

Early Encounters With The Grizzly

His actual acquaintance with the Old West began in 1885 when Stimson, at the age of 18, spent his first vacation in the Colorado Rockies. The last of his early visits to that area took place in 1890 when, with two companions, he traveled across the part of the Continental Range which lies between North Park on the east and Steamboat Springs on the west. Their pleasant sojourn in this beautiful country included a successful hunt, with a bag of five grizzlies and two black bears, besides the necessary meat for camp.

As Stimson gained hunting experience, he also began to realize the importance of having adequate arms. During the years between

1885 and 1890, he bought and used a number of repeating rifles. Because his 1890 Winchester 45/90 had a stock which did not fit his shoulder well, it caused him to shoot inaccurately at times, not to mention the fact that on one occasion he "lost a big grizzly bear owing to the lightness of the bullet." Even after getting the gun properly stocked, the defect of the lightness of the bullet still remained, and in 1894 he lost two more large grizzlies which apparently had been mortally wounded.

By that time he had come to realize that his chances of meeting grizzly bears would be mostly in the dusk when they were coming to a bait. Consequently, after a careful study of books on shooting, he decided that he ought to have a special rifle built for shooting grizzly bears in the dusk at bait. He visited the officers of the Winchester Company which had acquired the patents of the old Sharp rifle and they agreed to make him a single shot rifle of a caliber and power to correspond to those being made by English gun makers for use by Englishmen in hunting lions and tigers.

First Visit To Montana

When in 1891, he began to look for a wilder country than Colorado, he consulted George Bird Grinnell, the editor of *Field and Stream,* who told him:

> There is only one country that I know. It is situated in northwestern Montana near the Blackfoot Indian Reservation. It has never been explored or surveyed, and I am planning to go there myself next September to try to find the source of the St. Mary's River. That river comes out of the mountains into the Upper St. Mary's Lake and, so far as I know, no white man has ever visited its source. I suspect there are some big glaciers there. Would you like to go along with me?

Stimson needed no second invitation. The Pacific extension of the Great Northern Railway had not yet reached the Rocky Mountains when he and a classmate, William H. Seward, Jr., came west. They had to travel the last 150 miles by work train to the point where they were to meet Grinnell. With the latter and their guides, Billy Jackson*

---

*This is the same William Jackson described on page 7 of Chapter 1 and page 101 of Chapter 11.

and James Willard Schultz, they then moved northward by horse and wagon another 60 or 70 miles to Upper Lake St. Mary where their projected exploration was to begin.

Companions on St. Mary Trips

After that initial visit, Stimson came to northwestern Montana many times, although never alone. Sometimes he was accompanied by his wife Mabel, and by his sister; and on several occasions he was joined by his "dear college friend and earnest crusader for the preservation of the American forest, Gifford Pinchot, then Forester of the United States." At other times the party included Pinchot's brother, Amos, and two of Stimson's law partners, Bronson Winthrop and A.W. Putnam.

Of all his vacations, Stimson felt that the outing of 1897 in the region of Lake St. Mary and the Jackson Glacier was the most pleasant and successful. The party that year consisted of his wife, his sister and the two Pinchots. Horses and outfit for himself, wife and sister were furnished by H.A. Fox, "a fine old character who had been a member of the Seventh Cavalry at the Battle of the Little Big Horn, escaping Custer's Massacre because of having been assigned to the wagon train for that day." The Pinchots had with them Jack Munroe, "a former hunter and trapper who had married into the Blackfeet tribe." As Stimson tells the story in his *My Vacations*:

Old Rory

This trip in 1897 was a particularly lucky hunt for me. I was hunting for the first time with the two rifles that I had adopted: the big 577 single shot Winchester carrying three drams of black powder and some 600 grains of lead as my bear gun for close quarters with a grizzly; as well as the light single shot rifle which the Winchester Company had made as an experiment when they were competing for the United States Army's tests in the early '90s. This small rifle carried smokeless powder, the cartridge being the 30/40 caliber used then by the Army. Both rifles were equipped with Lyman sights, and the big rifle had a white ivory front sight for shooting in bad light.

Jack Munroe when he first joined us at once nicknamed my bear rifle 'Old Rory.' The lighter rifle, however, has been my principal reliance ever since except for close work at a grizzly bear. With it I have done all my other necessary shooting. Moose, elk, caribou, black bear, sheep, goats, deer, and British stags have all fallen before it. On this trip in 1897 I was lucky enough to get several mountain rams, a goat, and a grizzly bear.

In my shot at the bear, 'Old Rory' ended the series of failures I had had with less powerful rifles, and it was done under circumstances which gave me full confidence in the big gun. The bear was a large she bear coming rapidly to a bait which she was using. She had two good-sized cubs with her but they were not in sight as she loomed up into my vision. She came rapidly along the side of the mountain. Then when I raised from my hidden position and she saw me, she turned and all the hair on her back seemed to rise as she prepared for a charge. This was the only time I have ever had the threat of a bear's charge. But at the first shot she crumpled up and needed no more. The cubs then turned up, but I let them go. They were large enough to take care of themselves.

Characteristics Of The Big Bears

I have been asked why I consider the grizzly bear a dangerous animal to hunt. My answer is that while individual bears, like other individual animals, may differ somewhat in temperament, the grizzly bear has physical and racial characteristics well-known to those who have studied him which make him exceedingly dangerous to tamper with.

First, he is so ruggedly built and tenacious of life that he is very hard to kill — far more so than any other game animal on this continent and undoubtedly more so than any of the big cats abroad — the lion, the tiger, the leopard, etc. There are many recorded cases of a grizzly being shot through the lower end of the heart and yet charging home on his assailant.

This happened to Theodore Roosevelt in 1889 in Montana and he escaped the blow only by a lucky leap aside. It happened to Dr. Grinnell, the brother of my friend George Bird Grinnell in the St. Mary's country in Montana in the '90s. Dr. Grinnell was hunting with Jack Munroe and shot a rather small grizzly through the heart. She at once charged the two men, who backed away, each shooting at her with their repeating rifles until she finally fell dead at the feet of Munroe. I myself have knocked over with an ordinary repeating rifle at least four grizzlies which, though badly wounded, two undoubtedly fatally wounded, yet got up and got away from me.

Second, the immense power of the grizzly's blow. If he gets near enough to strike with his forepaw, you are gone. Many fullgrown cattle have been killed outright with that blow.

Third, his innate aggressive spirit. When his enemy, man, was armed only with the muzzle loading rifle of the early pioneer, the grizzly lorded it over the entire zone of his habitat. He lived and hunted by daylight, frequently attacking men and animals without provocation. He was largely carnivorous. He still eats flesh whenever he can get it.

The development of the modern heavy rifle, particularly the heavy smokeless powder rifle, has largely changed the grizzly's habits. He has become a very cautious nocturnal animal. It is very rare that he is seen in daylight or in the open. He is so cautious about the scent or noise of men that almost the only way a shot can be obtained is by watching a carcass which he is feeding on. Even then his scent for man is so keen that I have found it wise to arrange a method of approach by which the hunter waits at a distance until the bear has come to the bait in the dim light of the evening and then creeps up on him upwind.

The 1901 Safari

That is the method used in two cases which I mentioned in this book. But before I got the rifle which Jack Munroe christened "Old Rory," there were several occasions in which, if the bear had chosen to charge and not run away, I should probably not have come home. Since I obtained that rifle I have never lost a grizzly on which I used it.

In 1901 when I visited the Glacier camp again with my wife and sister and a friend from Squadron A, we were treated very differently by the weather than we had been in 1897. It rained and snowed and sleeted unceasingly in the Blackfoot basin until the entire basin and the whole of Mt. Jackson became covered with snow which made it indistinguishable from the glacier itself. In seasons like that there was not much fun, particularly for the ladies who went with us and who were cooped up in a smoky tepee most of the time. My friend got a mountain goat, and up to the end of the trip that was all, for I myself was not anxious for goats.

In an adjacent valley I had laid a bait for bear and a grizzly had found it. Night after night I watched that bait from the distant stalking point which we had selected to avoid giving our scent to the approaching bear, but nothing approached until it had grown so dark that I could see my sights no longer. Morning after morning I arose at

3 A.M. so as to cross the long distance that separated camp from the bait and reach the latter by daybreak, only to find that the bear had been there while the night was in the full.

The Long Wait

It came to the last day of our possible stay and there had been no change. I had only one night more and I decided that something desperate must be done. As usual I waited in the watching point until twilight came on and then I crawled down to a shooting point which was only twenty-two yards from the bait. The bait lay in a little mountain valley full of grass and scattered with small fir brushes. The shooting point which I chose was a long, low, flat rock just high enough when I lay upon it to raise my rifle above the surrounding grass.

There I determined to wait all night if necessary until my bear came. Gradually it grew completely dark. It was not a pleasant night. Although there was a moon, it was hidden by the clouds which showered driving snow and sleet upon us, leaving only just enough light to distinguish the open meadow from the little fir bushes which studded it here and there. Ten o'clock came. I had with me young Fox who carried my old 45/90. I suddenly noticed that one of the dark blurs which represented fir bushes began to move across the meadow from the woods bordering one side of it. It came up until it reached the bait and then elongated itself.

A Shot In The Dark

My bear had evidently come and turned broadside. I could not tell which was the front end and which the rear of the rectangle that stood before me. I could not see my sights or even the white cloth I had tied around my gun. But Old Rory had a round barrel and that barrel gave just enough gleam to show slightly in the dim light. I lay on my belly and sighted it as one would a field gun, first taking the glimmer on the top of the barrel and pointing it toward the end which I assumed to be the front end of the bear, then holding the gun perfectly still while I moved my head to the side and caught the gleam along the barrel on the side, and elevated that to the proper height to hit the rectangle.

Then I squeezed the trigger. There were two roars — first Old Rory, and then a roar from the bear which began throwing itself about in the dimness. It was mortally hit and would probably have died where it was if at that moment the nerves of young Fox, who had been lying behind me, had not given way. He leaped to his feet and began pumping cartridges from my 45/90 in the direction of the bear, with the only result that he drove the bear to get up and move across the meadow to the edge of the nearest fringe of woods into which he plunged. I with my single shot rifle fired another shot as he entered the woods, but when we afterwards found the bear, we found that neither my second shot nor any of Fox's had taken effect.

I was desperate and determined to mark him if I could before I left the place. In the valley in which we were, there was another meadow separated by the narrow strip of woods into which the bear had plunged. With my gun at a cock I pushed my way through the strip of woods in which we could see nothing and out into that further meadow. That meadow, like our own, was studded with small dark objects, one of which might well be the bear, and the others certainly were fir bushes. I pushed my way across it in the direction the bear had been moving, going up to each fir bush with my gun pointed until I could identify it.

The Morning After

We had progressed about half across the meadow when there came on our front, where there was another strip of woods, a snarling growl from the bear. Young Fox, who up to that moment had followed me with my gun, hissed in my ear that he wouldn't go another blank blank step. I agreed with him. We had found where our bear was and I was satisfied that, having lain down again, it would not go any further; we could come back in the morning and find it dead; and we did. Old Rory had done its work alone and the work was very thorough. I had fortunately guessed at the right end of the bear, and the bullet had ranged from the left foreshoulder back to the right rear flank.

Of course, what I had done in following the bear was dangerous. But I had grown so confident in my gun and so annoyed with the long disappointments of fruitless watching that I took the chance. I might say that if I had not followed it until I located it by that last snarl, it is quite possible that we would not have found it at all because the bear, although a full grown grizzly, had so buried itself in the ground and bushes under a low branch fir tree that it would have been very difficult to find him when we came back the next morning.

The next morning. Finding the dead grizzly. Stimson is on the left.

Adventure of 1907

On our next trip to Montana, we decided to explore some of the region south of our old St. Mary's country and south of the Great Northern Railway. This was an area which had not been visited by us, and where the range of the Rockies was somewhat lower than in our beautiful north. We hoped to escape the bad weather of the glacier region and to have the interest of seeing a new area. There was quite a party of us. My wife and I made the first start and we were to be joined a few days later by a group which included the Pinchot brothers, my junior partner, A.W. Putnam, and two friends from Squadron A — Frank Outerbridge and J. Harold Cram.

None of us had been in the country to be visited, which was the headwaters of Badger Creek which runs eastward from the mountains into the prairie. Jack Munroe was our guide, and he furnished another man as horse rustler and cook, whose name I do not remember. As it turned out, we saw more game than we had ever seen in the northern country and had an experience with an enterprising old grizzly which was interesting and in which the results were entirely in his favor.

Hiding The Hams

Mabel and I with Jack Munroe and the cook started up the creek to get some meat with which to greet the others when they came later. We moved about halfway up the creek and made a camp, and I was fortunate in getting fairly promptly a good bull elk which was brought into camp. Then followed a vigorous argument between Jack Munroe and myself as to how to preserve the hams of the elk so that they would keep while he went back and got the rest of the party and we waited a little further back where we could get a better camp. Jack was all for putting the entire cache up a big tree and letting it hang. While that is the traditional method of keeping meat in the drier southern Rockies, I was a little afraid that it would not keep here in the north where we had a damper climate. Furthermore, a black bear or sometimes a small grizzly can climb a tree if it is put to it.

I suggested that we follow a custom that I had heard of in eastern Canada of keeping meat under cold water. Jack pooh-poohed this and said that a bear would find it nonetheless. Finally we compromised. We hung one ham well up on a large tree near the camp site and placed the other in a large pool of Badger Creek which flowed past the camp site a short distance away. The pool was deep

The skin of the dead grizzly packed to take to camp. Figure is Stimson's sister.

enough to flow entirely over the ham and I thought would thus cut off any scent from the air.

Stalking A Grizzly

Jack then went back to his ranch to meet the rest of the party, and my wife and I with the other man also returned a short distance down where we found a good camp and waited. We waited a long time, much longer than had been the schedule. Finally as our supplies ran low, we determined to ride back to the prairie to find out what had happened. On the way we ran into the whole party coming up. We turned and joined them. With a party of seven and the pack horses it was a long train. Jack was leading and I took my place at the rear to keep the pack horses in line. When we had gotten within perhaps a mile of our original camp where the meat was, a messenger came down the pack line from Jack to me, pointing out the track of a big grizzly in the trail we were following, saying, 'Henry L., I told you so, he's got your meat.'

We stopped and consulted. I was very skeptical of the bear being at the meat or, if he was, being approachable by hunters in daylight. But we had friends in the party who had never hunted a bear and wanted to begin. I agreed to take Cram, who was one of the most eager, and as his guide go up with him on foot along the brook to the meat which was in the pool about a mile away and see if we could get a shot at the bear there; while Gifford Pinchot preceded the pack train on the trail on foot in order to try to get a shot at the bear if Cram and I started him and drove him toward the trail.

The brook and the trail ran parallel about two hundred yards apart. The others and the pack train were to let us get ahead and then follow slowly up the trail. Cram and I took up our course on the brook, he going ahead with his rifle and I whispering directions from behind. My experience with the alertness of bears in the woods made me very skeptical of our having any luck. I took with me my 30/40 rifle because it was the lighter to carry. I didn't think the bear was at the pool in the first place, and in the second place, if he was, I was confident he would hear us coming and steal away. The one thing I did not take into calculation and which completely changed the situation was that the brook, while small, was rather noisy, and masked the sound of our footsteps.

Interrupting A Siesta

The word was given and the complicated scheme was set in motion. Cram and I disappeared in the woods following the stream. In time we reached the pool where the meat had been hidden. On the opposite side from us and on the side toward the parallel trail was a rather steep clay bank about ten feet high. We approached the whole place with great caution and looked into the pool. The meat had been taken. We could see nothing around the pool. There was no noise or motion.

We went down to the bank of the pool to see if there were any tracks visible, Cram still proceeding and I following. Our quiet search took us under the high bank. I suddenly heard a slight snort above my head and looking up I saw peering at me through the grass at the top and not more than ten feet away from my head the head of a big grizzly who had evidently been lying asleep after a thoroughly satisfactory meal. The head was immediately withdrawn.

I made a running climb of the bank as fast as I could to try to get a shot. Cram had not heard the bear's snort and could not understand what I was doing. The bank was fairly steep and by the time that I reached the top I just got a glimpse of our bear sailing through the woods on a round canter over in the direction where I hoped Pinchot would be. I took a shot through the brush at the bear but without effect. The bear did not connect with Pinchot but did connect with the pack train coming up the trail a short distance behind, and for a few moments there was a wild scatteration of horses and riders.

But the old boy got away unharmed. When I examined his nest, I found it a good one, hidden in the grass. He had dragged the ham up there and had eaten it all and had then been taking a comfortable siesta to digest it. Needless to repeat what Jack Munroe said to me thereafter about preserving meat in water! His ham in the tree was still safe.

Grizzly Aggressiveness

Before leaving the story of *My Vacations,* it should be noted that Stimson had characterized the grizzly as an "innate aggressive spirit," living and hunting, when it had only the muzzle loading rifle to fear, "by daylight, *frequently attacking men and animals without provocation.*"

While his statement had reference to early days in the Old West, it was given as one of the reasons why the grizzly was a dangerous animal to hunt during the years (1885-1907) when he was actively hunting it. Had these assertions been made during the lifetime of grizzly expert William H. Wright and had they come to his attention, he would certainly have taken exception to their accuracy, for all the reasons outlined in Chapter 8, *supra*.

The curious thing about Stimson's statement as to grizzly aggressiveness is that it was not borne out by his own experience. The only glimpses he ever had of grizzlies in the Montana Rockies were of bears that fled at his approach — usually bears that had been feeding on the carcass of some animal killed by a hunter for bait, or otherwise deceased. As a matter of fact, the big bears were so shy and elusive that he could find no way to get within shooting range of one except by the use of bait, and even then daytime confrontations were the exception, rather than the rule. Never had he been charged by any of the grizzlies that he encountered during his hunting career.

Hiker standing near Dawson Pass, overlooking Two Medicine Lake, 8 miles away and more than 2300 feet below.

XI

THE MEDICINE GRIZZLY
OF CUT BANK CANYON

The Cut Bank Valley is situated on the east side of Glacier Park, with St. Mary to the north and Two Medicine to the south. Although it has no sizeable lake, a sturdy stream runs through it, carrying away the melting snows from Triple Divide and Cut Bank Passes. Through it led the old Blackfoot war trail, used in the early days, when the Indians crossed the Rockies on war expeditions against the Pend d'Oreille, Kutenai and Flathead tribes.

It was great hunting country around the turn of the century, and Walter McClintock tells, in his book *The Old North Trail,* how he and his friend William Jackson* followed the trail with their pack horses, into the valley in search of game. Jackson's Blackfoot name was Siksikakoan, and he was a grandson of the legendary Hugh Monroe, known as the "White Blackfoot." Like his grandfather, Jackson spent much time in and near what is now Glacier Park. He had visited the Cut Bank Valley many times.

An Unexpected Visitor

As McClintock tells the story, the two men had reached the end of a long day's trek, and proceeded to turn their horses loose to feed while Jackson built a small fire for cooking and warmth. They felt secure in turning the horses loose near camp because of rich pastur-

---

*This is the same William Jackson described at page 2 of Chapter 1 and page 76 of Chapter 10.

age, and the weariness of the animals. Suddenly they heard a loud snorting and a clatter of hoofs as the horses galloped madly through the clearing. Hurrying to discover the cause of the panic, the men found among the horse tracks huge footprints of a grizzly bear. Apparently it had been feasting on huckleberries, tearing up the ground, and turning over large stones for insects.

In the words of McClintock, after they had returned to their campfire, Siksikakoan said:

I once had an experience with a bear in this same locality so unusual, that the bear himself can hardly have forgotten it. It was in the early spring, about the time when bears leave their winter dens. I had followed so long and eagerly the fresh trail of a large mountain ram that nightfall overtook me unprepared. The weather luckily was warm and pleasant. Finding a depression in the ground filled with long soft grass, I stood my rifle against a neighboring tree and lay down in the hollow place to sleep.

During the night I was aroused by the heavy breathing of a large animal, and an oppressive and disagreeable odor. At first, I was dazed and only half conscious, as in a dream, of something standing over me, but I lay perfectly still. A grunting and snuffing, close by my head, quickly forced me to realize that I was in the strange and horrible predicament of lying beneath a grizzly bear.

A cold sweat came over me, and I was half paralyzed with terror. The grizzly had been prowling about, led to my bed by his scent of the remnants of my supper, and so happened to walk over my body, partly covered by the grass and hidden in the depression.

It was of course impossible to reach my rifle standing against the tree. Acting on a sudden impulse, I doubled up my knees, and with all my strength plunged my fists and feet simultaneously against the body of the brute. It was a complete surprise for the grizzly, who was, if possible, the more frightened of the two, for he ran bellowing into the forest, while I quickly gathered up my small outfit and started away in the dark.

Glimpsing A Grizzly

On the following morning, while Siksikakoan was examining the surrounding heights for game, he caught sight of a band of Rocky Mountain sheep quietly feeding above timberline. While he was considering the best way of approaching them, the band suddenly took flight. Then a dark figure appeared with awkward gait, following the sheep over the boulders. McClintock's glasses showed it to be a large grizzly bear. Siksikakoan said: "It is our old friend of last evening," and seizing his rifle called to McClintock to follow him. They climbed the mountain facing them, crawling through thick underbrush and scaling difficult ledges. In one place they discovered the grizzly's freshly made tracks in the soft earth beside a small stream. But the excitement over their seeming proximity to the monster was of short duration. When they reached the timberline, Siksikakoan stopped and said dejectedly: "The wind has shifted and old grizzly is gone." For McClintock, however, the announcement was one of great relief.

The two men, after unsuccessfully hunting for a couple of days, came upon a camp of two lodges belonging to Bird-Rattle and Looking-For-Smoke, who reported they had bagged six sheep. This meant the game had been frightened away from that vicinity, so it was decided that Siksikakoan would go among higher peaks at the head of the canyon while McClintock stayed in camp to guard the provisions and outfit.

Unwelcome Visitor

During the two or three days that Siksikakoan was gone, McClintock busied himself about camp, using his camera to photograph some of the beautiful landscapes along the old war trail that skirted camp. One night, as he lay under his warm blankets in the lodge, he fell into a doze but had a vague feeling that something was prowling about. Presently, upon hearing heavy footsteps nearby, he sat up and listened. They led in the direction of the kitchen some twenty feet away, and there followed a rattling of pans. As McClintock tells the story:

> I seized a stick and ran out to investigate. I saw a large, black-looking object nearby, and thinking that one of the horses had returned, was about to hurl my club. But a sudden intuition changed my mind. This intruder could not be a horse. It stood too high in front and low behind. It looked steadily at me with head lowered and moving slowly from side to side.
>
> When I heard a vicious 'woof!' the terrible reality flashed over me that I was in close quarters with a huge grizzly bear. The thought of

having come so near charging upon him with a club made me shudder and my knees feel weak. A cold chill crept up my back and over my scalp, with the feeling that my hair was standing on end. I backed into the lodge and sat down, debating what could be done.

I realized that in such close quarters and with a large grizzly at night, and with an inferior rifle, my large rifle having been taken by Siksikakoan, it would be madness to shoot. A bold front is the best defense, and to run from a grizzly is to invite attack. Any further deliberation was cut short by his moving toward the lodge. He stopped for an instant a few feet away, sniffing the scent of the provisions stored inside the lodge, but fortunately turned again toward the kitchen.

Believing that the firelight might drive him off, I cut a few shavings and soon revived my smouldering fire. Hearing him coming again, I seized the small rifle and jumped to the side farthest from him. While I stood waiting, the suspense and strain upon my nerves were terrible. He came straight to the lodge door, but again turned aside to investigate my saddles. His curiosity being satisfied, he stopped at the side of the lodge where our provisions were stored. I cocked the rifle and knelt in readiness to receive him.

Rising on his hind legs, he placed his fore paws against the lodge poles. I saw the canvas pressed in with his weight, and heard his deep breathing, for I was underneath him. I had now recovered my nerve. My heart beat steadily and I held the rifle without a tremor, although I thought my end had surely come.

Making A Shambles Of The Kitchen

I quickly loosened the canvas from its pegs and prepared to escape from under, for I thought his weight would break through. But he stood there sniffing the air and seemingly undecided as to his next move. Then I stood erect and gave a loud yell. He must have thought my 'power' was stronger than his own, for he turned away and the next moment I heard him at the kitchen, tearing off the canvas covering from a mess of trout.

Having safely passed through what I thought was the crisis of his visit, I actually began to take a friendly interest in the old grizzly's performances, and watched him from the doorway. He tore open the parfleches containing flour and sugar and smelled at the heavy iron 'dutch-oven' containing a small piece of butter, my greatest delicacy, although not very fresh. He turned the oven over and over, but the lid held fast. Finally he gave it a heavy blow with his big fore paw, and the lid flew off. Its contents were quickly disposed of and I heard his rough tongue licking with relish the inside of the kettle.

With the hope that I might drive him away, I opened the lodge door that the firelight might show more brightly, and stepping out fired my rifle into the air. But he only threw up his head, as if annoyed by the interruption, and dropped it quickly to finish a bowl of stewed peaches, the last of my store of provisions at the kitchen.

When the first faint streaks of dawn appeared, my dangerous visitor suddenly departed into the deep forest. Having built a cheerful and comfortable fire, I at once wrote in my notebook the details of the grizzly's visit and then, wrapping myself in my blankets, slept soundly until wakened by the squirrels racing over the frozen canvas above my head.

The thrilling events of the night seemed like a dream and I hastened to find the grizzly's tracks and prove the reality of the adventure. Close beside the lodge, I found prints of his feet measuring thirteen inches in length, six inches broad at the heel and seven inches across the toes. When Siksikakoan returned, bringing a Rocky Mountain sheep and two goats, he said that a grizzly of that size would weigh as much as a large horse.

That evening, while seated beside our outside fire, after telling about his hunt, Siksikakoan said:

We are now camped within the range of a grizzly bear who has been famous for many years among the Blackfeet for his size and daring. I will tell you the story, just as Mad Wolf told it to me.

Legend of the Medicine Grizzly

When Mad Wolf was a young man, he was chief of a war party that crossed the Rocky Mountains against the Flathead Indians. Two of his brothers also started with the expedition, but turned back before they reached the Flathead country. Mad Wolf and his party returned later by the Cut Bank Pass. After crossing the summit, they entered the dense forest near the head of the canyon. Mad Wolf was in the lead, while the others followed in two separate columns along each side of the trail, as was the custom of war parties in those days.

They rode in silence because the trees were so dense they could not see far in advance. Suddenly Mad Wolf stopped and signed to the others that he heard some one ahead striking his horse with a quirt. The Blackfeet quickly ambushed themselves among the trees. A war party of Kutenai (Mountain) Indians were returning from an expedition into the Blackfeet country. They ran into the ambush and there was a fierce battle.

Mad Wolf, as chief of the expedition, was entitled to the first shot. He singled out the leader, but the Kutenai chief was very brave. Although badly wounded, he ran into the thick woods where Mad Wolf killed him. While taking his scalp, Mad Wolf recognized on his belt the scalps of his own two brothers. He hurried back to his people, who were by this time hard pressed by the Kutenai and were retreating.

Mad Wolf, now aroused to great courage and daring, rallied the Blackfeet to another attack and soon turned the rout into a victory. They killed all of the Kutenais save one old squaw. After scalping the dead, they clothed her in a soft tanned buckskin dress, ornamented with elk teeth and with leggings and moccasins decorated with porcupine quills. They painted her face black and giving her a warm blanket and a sack of dried meat, set her free, with the prayer that the Sun would take pity on themselves, just as they had pitied their helpless enemy.

The Camp By The Big Fir Tree

They then continued on their way until they came upon the camp of Running Wolf, Black Bear, Ear Rings, Stock-stchi, Ahpasis, and other well-known Blackfeet chiefs pitched in this same glade near yonder big fir tree, by which our people have ever since identified this camping ground.

It was in early summer, the time when the camas is in bloom and they were engaged in cutting and peeling lodge poles. In those days the Blackfeet traveled so far in a year that their lodge poles were worn too short. Every spring they went into the mountains to cut new poles and to dig camas roots.

It happened that in the evening the chiefs were assembled in Stock-stchi's lodge, listening to Mad Wolf's story of his war expedition against the Flatheads. It was a warm moonlight night and the women were sitting outside singing and talking together. Stock-stchi called to his wife to go to the stream for water. But she was afraid, saying, 'The woods are dark down there and the water deep.' But her husband made her go. She soon returned, badly frightened, and said:

'I was dipping my bucket, when a man came from the forest. He jumped across the stream and ran up the trail. He carried a rifle and wore a war bonnet.'

Just then another woman came into the lodge saying:

We saw a stranger go to the big fir tree yonder. He hung his war bonnet there and then stole over to the lodge. He looked in and went away. He was an enemy. We saw him plainly in the bright moonlight.'

Mad Wolf and the other chiefs hurriedly seized their rifles and ran down to the stream just in time to see a small party of Gros Ventres emerging from the forest. The Blackfeet opened fire and killed all except their leader. He stood his ground until his ammunition gave out, when he took refuge in the underbrush.

Our people clipped the branches off all around him with their bullets, but could not hit him. Finally they made a charge, but the Gros Ventre chief fought savagely with his knife, roaring all the time like a grizzly bear at bay and calling to the Blackfeet —

'Come on, I am not afraid. My name is A-koch-kit-ope and my medicine is powerful.' When day broke, our people were uneasy, thinking the Gros Ventre chief might have supernatural power. They told him he was free to go, but they would scalp the others. A-koch-kit-ope replied, 'No, they are my brothers and I will not leave them.'

A-koch-kit-ope Becomes A Grizzly

Feeling thirsty, he walked to the river and drank, daring any of the Blackfeet to stand forth for a hand-to-hand conflict. When our people finally killed him, they discovered that the grizzly bear was his medicine. He had a grizzly claw tied in his front hair. The Blackfeet were so afraid that some of his power might escape, that they built a fire and burned A-koch-kit-ope's body. If a spark or coal flew out, they carefully threw it back into the fire to prevent the possible escape of any of his power. They scalped the other dead Gros Ventres and had a scalp dance around the fire.

When the fire had burned out, the Blackfeet hurriedly moved camp. But in spite of their precautions, A-koch-kit-ope transformed himself into an enormous grizzly bear and followed them. He came upon the Blackfeet when they were pitching camp, killing some, while the rest escaped by flight.

The next spring when our people were up the canyon to cut lodge poles, they camped again near the big fir tree in the same park. Early in the night, while the horses were still picketed close to the lodges, an enormous grizzly bear came into camp. The horses were frightened and stampeded, just as ours have done. The dogs attacked him, and he killed some of them and put the others to flight. The people were afraid to shoot, because they recognized the bear as A-koch-kit-ope. He appeared beside the fir tree, where the year before the Gros Ventre medicine man had hung his war bonnet.

The grizzly went boldly through camp eating all of the food he found and tearing to pieces hides and parfleches. Whenever our people camp near the fir tree in the canyon they see the medicine grizzly, whom they have named A-koch-kit-ope. He comes only at night and disappears before daybreak. The Blackfeet know his medicine is strong and are afraid to shoot at him.

When we made peace with the Gros Ventres, we told them about this medicine grizzly and they said that he was A-koch-kit-ope, their great medicine man. They declared he could not have been killed, if all his followers had not been slain first. A-koch-kit-ope had predicted to them that he would be killed if he should ever be left alone in battle with no one to make a 'medicine smoke.' As this happened many years ago, A-koch-kit-ope, the medicine grizzly, must now be very old.

McClintock Ponders The Legend

After Siksikakoan had finished telling the legend of the Medicine Grizzly, his young companion went out into the night. He gazed with a deeper interest at the big fir tree, where the Gros Ventre warrior hung his war bonnet, while making the night attack upon the Blackfeet, and at the black, wall-like line of forest, where the Blackfoot woman first encountered A-koch-kit-ope. He felt that the huge grizzly which had frightened him the night before must be the dreaded "Medicine Grizzly, A-koch-kit-ope," who had already made that locality famous by so many manifestations of his supernatural power.

Beyond were the massive mountains, their snowy summits dimly lighted by myriads of brightly shining stars. In the northeast the dog star rose with remarkable brilliancy over the tops of tall spruces and pines. The horses could be faintly distinguished at the edge of the timber, one of them giving a frightened whinny when it suddenly realized that it was feeding alone, too near the ghostly woods, and hurriedly rejoined its companions. Returning to the lodge, he turned into his comfortable blanket-bed beside the fire, and listened as the stillness of the night was broken only by the mournful howl of a wolf

96

in the forest close by.

McClintock's adventure with the Medicine Grizzly took place around the turn of the century. The monster bear continued to haunt the area and its reputation spread far and wide until the stories about it grew to fabulous proportions. Great medicine or power was ascribed to the animal by the Blackfeet who were loath to go into the valley because of its presence.

End Of The Monster Grizzly

Some members of the *Ursus arctos* clan must enjoy exceptional longevity, for a giant grizzly was still conducting its reign of terror in Cut Bank Valley a full two decades after McClintock's hair-raising adventure. But the special protection it enjoyed as a national park inhabitant came to an end in the early 1920's when the Park Service adopted a policy of predator control directed at reducing the numbers of the Park's carnivores, thus to provide what was thought to be much needed protection for such gentler creatures as deer, sheep and goats.

Cut Bank Valley was chosen as the locale for the initiation of this long-since obsolete program. The man selected for the job was "Chance" Beebe, a lion hunter for the United States Biological Survey, who had formerly served as a Glacier Park ranger at St. Mary. In the course of his Cut Bank campaign, Chance is said to have established a record of 67 scalps, but his greatest trophy was the pelt of the monster Cut Bank grizzly. He finally slew the creature after an exciting campaign of relentless pursuit in which man and beast matched wits and interchanged roles in stalking each other.

Presumably the bear that Beebe killed was the same Medicine Grizzly that had terrorized the Blackfeet, and had given Siksikakoan's young companion a fright around the turn of the century. We know, of course, that grizzlies are no longer a problem in the valley of the Cut Bank; and we also know that the existence of its most extraordinary inhabitant has been commemorated by the names given to Medicine Grizzly Lake, six miles above the Cut Bank Campground, and to Medicine Grizzly Peak, rising to an elevation of 8315 feet near the Continental Divide.

Mother bear with her two subadult grizzly cubs.

XII

GRIZZLY FEMMES FATALES

From the pen of Kipling came the immortal cliche' that the female of the species is more deadly than the male. It is an aphorism that has particular application to the world of animals, where female gorillas are usually more dangerous and aggressive than males, where the lady lion is frequently the killer of game for the family, and where the mother grizzly is a fierce defender of her offspring.

Whether the setting be Glacier National Park in British Columbia or Glacier National Park in Montana, the reactions and behavior of a female grizzly accompanied by her cubs are likely to be very much the same. Under the title "No Time For Fear," the Reader's Digest for April, 1976 told the poignant story of a boy, a girl, and an enraged grizzly.

The Grizzly Of Balu Pass

On October 1, 1971, while Malcolm Aspeslet, 19, and Barb Beck, 18, were on a hike to Balu Pass, 6700 feet up in the Glacier National Park of Canada they were caught by an early snow storm, and had to spend the night in a cabin near the summit. Descending the icy trail the next morning, they unexpectedly encountered a mother grizzly and her two cubs. When she attacked Barb, Malcolm unhesitatingly pulled a hunting knife from his belt and slashed desperately at the great bear with little effect except to direct her fury at him.

After mauling him unmercifully, the grizzly departed with her cubs, and Barb, though badly wounded, hastened to the lodge below for help. When the rescue party arrived, they found that Malcolm's scalp had been torn off, the right side of his face had been peeled back to reveal muscle and sinew, one eye was nearly severed, a wrist was broken, one kneecap was torn off, and both legs had suffered great gashes. Surgery at Revelstoke required seven hours and more than 1,000 stitches. Forty-one skin-graft operations were performed over a period of months in the effort to restore his appearance. The results were somewhat discouraging, and Malcolm became despondent that Barb could ever feel anything but pity for him.

Bravest Deed Of The Year

But the story had a happy ending. During leap year, Barb proposed that they be married and the wedding took place on July 21, 1973. In the meantime, word of his heroic exploit spread over Canada. Malcolm received the gold medal for bravery from the Royal Canadian Humane Association, the Carnegie Medal for heroism from the Carnegie Hero Fund Commission, and the Stanhope Gold Medal from the Royal Humane Society, London, for performing the bravest deed reported that year in the entire Commonwealth. Finally, he was chosen for the Canadian Government's Star of Courage which he received from Queen Elizabeth herself during her state visit to Canada.

Today Barb and Malcolm live in Surrey, near Vancouver, where he runs the kitchen at the Surrey Inn and she has an office job. His twisted facial features are being improved by surgery each year, and doctors have restored his injured eye, although he still has trouble using it. What happened to the lady grizzly that perpetrated the attack is not related in the story of Barb and Malcolm, although it illustrates the fact that raw courage alone is a wholly inadequate defense against the power of such a beast.

The Grizzly and The Doctor

One of the most unusual bear stories of all time appeared in a book entitled *Hunting and Conservation* published in 1925 by the Yale University Press, for which George Bird Grinnell was one of the editors. The author of the autobiographical article was Dr. Charles

B. Penrose, brother of the distinguished United States Senator Boies Penrose from Pennsylvania. It was entitled "An Encounter With A Grizzly Bear" and read as follows:

On September 1, 1907, my brothers Boies and Spencer and I had made a camp in the mountains lying between the Middle and South Forks of the Flathead River in Montana — about 5 miles south of the line of the Great Northern Railroad. The country was very rough and difficult of access, and we saw no signs of man having been there before, except the recent trail of a small party of the U.S. Geological Survey in charge of Mr. A.L. Stiles, who had gone there to map the country. Our camp was situated nearly on top of the range, at this place about 7,000 feet. The highest neighboring peaks were under 8,000 feet. The Geological party was camped about a mile away.

At 4 o'clock in the afternoon, I rode out with Mr. Stiles to see if we could get a deer. About two miles from camp, we tied up the horses and set out separately to hunt on foot. I walked along a rocky ridge covered with scattering burnt timber, and when about half a mile from where we started, a small grizzly appeared about 75 yards off, coming toward me. He was unaware of me and his head was down nosing the ground. I shot at him and he ran and rolled down the side of the ridge about 200 yards and fell dead beside a small creek. I fired two more shots at him as he ran. The country was open; nothing but masses of rock and naked burnt trees. No other bear was visible.

I went down to the small stream beside which the bear had fallen, put my gun against a tree, and was about to take out my pocket knife to skin him, when two grizzlies — one smaller than the other — suddenly appeared on the side of the ridge about 30 yards away. They had previously been concealed from my view by the irregularity of the rocky ground.

The Mother Bear Attacks

The larger bear took in the situation instantly. The hair of her back became erect, she growled, crouched, and came for me at a lope. As soon as I saw her, I jumped for my gun and was able to fire two shots before she was on me, the last shot just as she grabbed me. She did not rear up or strike with her paws, but came at me like a dog and seized with her teeth the mass of muscles in front of the left thigh. This threw me on my back, in the creek, and the gun fell from my hand. She shook the leg as a terrier does a rat, then seized and crushed my left wrist; then took hold of the right breast and pulled and shook it.

101

She stopped suddenly and stood over me growling. For a few seconds I lay still, then reached for the gun lying beside me.

Thereupon she started again and tried to chew the top of my head through the felt hat, making several wounds in the skull. She then chewed the right side of my face and neck, one of her canine teeth going through the cheek and breaking off one of my teeth. I thought I was 'all in' and was impressed by the painlessness of the proceeding, and recalled the experience of Livingstone, who wrote that he suffered no pain at all when he was attacked and chewed by a lion. Again she stopped, and this time I made no movement. She stood there some seconds, then turned, crossed the little creek, walked up the opposite bank about 20 yards, and fell dying against a tree stump. I saw the blood flowing from the left hip and knew that one of the shots had mortally wounded her.

I recovered my gun and got up and aimed at the third bear, which had been meanwhile standing where I first saw him, growling and whining and with the hair of his back erect. The gun snapped and on throwing open the chamber, I found that there was no cartridge in it. I felt for an extra cartridge in my trousers pocket but found none; the two or three that had been there were gone, having dropped out in the scuffle. But the bear did not wait. He turned and with plaintive howls loped off down the ridge.

Aftereffects Of The Attack

I was unaware of the extent of my injuries and felt no pain, weakness or shock. I was soaked with water from the creek and was covered with my own blood and that of the bear. I sat down to examine the wounds; felt my pulse, which was good; and found that there was no serious bleeding. The only serious injury was that of the left wrist, which was crushed, and from which a fragment of bone projected. I washed my handkerchief in the stream, wrapped it about the wrist, and walked back to the horses. Here I met Mr. Stiles and together we returned to camp.

I had in camp dressings, bichloride of mercury, and instruments and I carefully dressed the wounds, took a quarter of a grain of morphine hypodermatically and got into my sleeping bag.

The next morning we started at 7 o'clock, and under the guidance of Mr. Stiles made for the Great Northern Railroad, about 4,000 feet below us, and not many miles away in a straight line, but much further as we were obliged to travel. There was no trail, and the country was very precipitous and rough — snow banks, slide rock, fallen timber and underbrush. Much axe work was necessary to get through the fallen timber and underbrush. During most of the journey riding was impossible. We were all day at it, and it was nine o'clock at night when we dropped down to the Great Northern station at Nyack. The stationmaster and his wife, the only inhabitants of Nyack, gave us supper. In the morning we flagged the train going east and started for home.

The Two Dead Bears

The day after this occurrence one of the men whom we had left at camp skinned and examined the bear, and from his report I find that the bear that mauled me had been hit twice. One ball, entering behind the left shoulder and ranging backward, emerged from the left hip, probably cutting the femoral artery in its course. The other shot had broken a hind leg near the paw. The bear evidently bled to death.

The bear first killed was a good-sized two-year-old — two years old the previous spring. The bear that attacked me was the mother. Cubs often stay with the mother two years or longer if she fails to have cubs in the meantime. The young one was old enough to take care of itself and in the past I had shot bears of the same size, unaccompanied by the mother. When I shot I thought it was merely a small grizzly traveling alone. It did not occur to me that other members of the family might be about, or I would have looked out for them. The little bear was in the lead; the mother and the other two-year-old being behind and hidden by the irregular ground. When they struck the trail of the young one that had been shot, they followed down the side of the ridge until we saw each other.

The mother was about a 300-pound bear, and all three of them were unusually white in color — the whitest grizzlies I have ever seen.

The mother attacked me because I had killed her young and because she had not learned to fear man. She had probably never seen man before. She was in an inaccessible country, rarely if ever visited by man. A bear will not always fight for her cub. I have several times seen a black bear run away while her cub was being killed; and though the grizzly is much fiercer than the black, I think that she also would run after having become familiar with man and his weapons. In the early days, grizzlies often attacked man, though unmolested; now they usually get away as soon as they become aware that man is near.

Afterthoughts Of The Doctor

An interesting point in this experience is that the bear did not rear when attacking, nor did she strike with her paws. There was no claw wound. The wounds were all made by the teeth. Perhaps the injury to her hind leg prevented her rearing.

Another point of interest is the absence of pain during the encounter. Much sympathy is wasted on the imagined suffering of wounded men. Every surgeon knows that acute traumatism is usually painless. The soldier is often unaware that he is shot. Numerous hunters have recorded the absence of pain when chewed or gored by wild animals.

I had 30 tooth wounds. The muscles of the thigh were crushed and lacerated; the wrist joint was open, several of the small bones were crushed and the scaphoid bone was bitten in two, one fragment projecting from the wound. The median nerve was severed at the wrist; the hand had been perforated by teeth in several places; the breast, head, cheek and neck were bitten; and yet when I got up to take a shot at the last bear I felt no pain and was unaware of any injury.

I do not think that I fought back when the bear was chewing me. The attack was sudden, too sudden to feel fear. The whole thing lasted but a very short time. I had no weapons but the gun (a 7MM Mauser) and a clasp knife in my pocket. The bare hands of a man are frail against a bear, and the man feels his complete helplessness to oppose such superior strength. It is like a dog with a rabbit.

Names On The Map

For many years I had carried in camp a surgical kit, but had never had occasion to use it except for trifling injuries. This time I needed it badly. I sterilized and dressed the wounds most carefully, spending three hours at it. The result was that there was no infection and no sepsis; most of the wounds healed without suppuration and the final recovery was unaccompanied by physical impairment or disability of any account.

To this day the U.S. Geological Survey maps of the area where the doctor's adventure occurred show Mt. Penrose as the name of the great peak lying almost directly south of Nyack, and Rescue Creek as the name of the stream that drains its northern slopes, and down which it was necessary for him to struggle to get back to the railroad.

104

Since Mr. Stiles, the man who had assisted the wounded doctor down the mountain, was the chief of a party then engaged in mapping the area for the Geological Survey, it is not difficult to surmise how both the peak and the creek received their names.

The Grizzly and The Professor

J. Gordon Edwards, Professor of Entomology at the California University at San Jose and author of *A Climber's Guide to Glacier National Park* has spent more than 20 summers in the Park, several of them as seasonal ranger and ranger naturalist. Much of that time was spent in climbing the Park's great peaks, as well as on and off its hundreds of miles of trails. But it was not until a fateful day in July, 1975 that he had the misfortune to encounter a lady grizzly which, as he says with rather grim humor, insisted on holding his hand. In his own words, here is the story:

I was alone, bushwacking up a steep hillside near Feather Plume Falls, when an awesome commotion exploded in the bushes and small trees about 50 feet away. The shrill yipping convinced me I had frightened a couple of bear cubs and I stopped quickly, anticipating an attack by the mother. I heard her snarling and bawling, but she wasn't visible to me. Soon the cubs were heard retreating, still yipping, and I relaxed and prepared to continue my climb. Suddenly I heard the sow returning, still snarling and bawling, and soon she appeared, bounding toward me through the tall bushes... and I was appalled to discover that she was a grizzly!

It was so incredible that I simply couldn't believe it was really happening, and perhaps that is why I felt no fear. I stood there thinking 'she'll know I'm not afraid, and she'll know I mean no harm, so she will veer off and return to her cubs,' There was an unfortunate divergence of opinion about that, and she quickly closed the gap between us with no hesitation whatever. When she was only a few feet away I instinctively raised my ice ax, placed the pointed end of the handle in the bear's chest, stepped backward, and shoved as hard as I could. She had very poor footing on these bushes, and it was surprising but gratifying to see her rolling down the steep hill. I thought 'now she will go away and leave me alone.' Again I was wrong! She came slowly back up the hill, one leap at a time, pausing to inspect me between leaps.

When she was close enough I again placed the ax handle in her chest, but then something went wrong. I was knocked violently backwards. My left hand flipped out before me as I lurched backward, and the bear grabbed it between her jaws. Fearing she would stand up and swat me with her powerful forelegs, I dropped the ice ax and fell to my knees right in front of the grizzly, yanking on my hand. She shifted her grip several times, yet I couldn't get my hand out of her mouth. I kept gently slapping her on top of the nose and around the eyes, while quietly saying, 'come on, let go, I won't hurt you' (as though I could!!!)

I meanwhile kept watching my fingers extending from the side of her mouth, abstractly hoping I wouldn't see them drop off... but she never did bite down hard on my hand. After 30 or 40 seconds of tugging back and forth my hand suddenly came free. I had a blurred glimpse of a bloody mess, and feared extensive bleeding. I instantly decided to test the validity of the stories I had heard so often during my many summers in the Park, to the effect that bears will not bother you (usually) if you 'play dead.'

Without hesitating I therefore fell on my face in front of the grizzly, with my back toward her. While falling, I raised my hands above my head and crossed my wrists with the hope that I could press hard enough to slow the bleeding I anticipated in that tangled left hand.

The sow went crazy behind me, snarling and bawling horrendously, dashing a few feet, then dashing back to stand over me, then going a bit further away, then returning quickly. After seven or eight of these retreats and returns, I heard her breaking off little trees about 30 feet away, and when she failed to return within a few seconds I slowly looked up. She was nowhere in sight!! Hastily I picked up my camera and ice ax and plowed straight down through the brush to the bottom of the hill, then raced downstream to the trail.

There I felt so safe that I held up my chewed hand and took several pictures of it, then hiked the 1½ miles to Josephine Lake to await the afternoon sightseeing launch. Within an hour after the attack I was aboard the launch and the rangers had been notified by radio. In another hour I had reached camp, picked up my wife and our car, and had driven to the excellent medical clinic in Cardston, Alberta. Two nurses and three doctors worked me over there, shoved the fatty extrusions back into the puncture wounds, and closed them with 14 stitches.

When I arrived back at camp, I found I had become a local hero, and at the "Christmas Party" at Many Glacier Hotel that night (July 25th) I was more in demand than Santa Claus. Next day the news media carried the story across the nation, and even Paul Harvey discussed the incident. I received calls from Hawaii, New Jersey, Indiana, Idaho, Oregon, Washington, Ohio and other states, asking how I was (news accounts failed to indicate how minor the injuries were).

Friends in San Jose mailed me the front page of the *San Jose Mercury* with a banner headline: 'BEAR RIPS SJS PROF,' and a smaller heading 'Plays Possum, Lives.' I knew then that I was in for a lot of kidding when I got home again and my friends and colleagues saw that I could still wiggle my fingers, and subsequent events bore that out. I got jokes, cartoons, homemade poems about me and the bear, and a great many cards and letters. Shortly after classes began, I found a bumper strip on my car one morning, reading —
WORLD'S OLDEST LIVING BEAR WRESTLER.'
I have left that strip on the bumper because I think it amuses the students, but I guess I also enjoy it because of that third word.

The bear encounter was an interesting experience, but I hope it was the last one! In the future I'll be making a lot more noise while bushwhacking, and I suspect I'll also be worrying a great deal more than I ever did before. Meanwhile, when people ask me (as they have hundreds of times in past years) what to do if they encounter a grizzly, I have no idea what to tell them!

The Grizzly of Okotomi Lake*

High in the heart of Glacier Park, Montana lies a beautiful mountain tarn called Okotomi (Yellowfish) Lake, so named by George Bird Grinnell for a part Blackfoot Indian who accompanied him on some of his early expeditions to the region. The lake lies six miles east of the continental divide and only five miles north of the celebrated Going-To-The-Sun-Highway.

The five-mile hike from Rising Sun Campground to the lake is a popular one. The trail is scenic, the fishing at the lake excellent; and so it happened that a group of hikers headed for the lake on Monday, July 18, 1960. Two of them were seasonal Park Rangers, Alan Nelson, 27, and Edomo Mazzer, 28, using their day off for hiking and fishing. A third was Smith (Smitty) Parratt, aged 10, youngest son of another seasonal ranger-naturalist from Upland, California who, with his family, was in the Park for the summer. Smitty often

---

*Adapted from *Attacked by a Grizzly*, Albert Ruffin, *Life*, ©1965 Time, Inc.

accompanied Nelson and Mazzer on their leisure-time hikes.

The three of them had come to the Rising Sun Campground that morning in Mazzer's car, which they parked there while they made their way up the trail. Somewhere along the route they had encountered two other hikers, Gote Myhlen, 42, and Miss Brita Noring, 38, vacationing Swedish schoolteachers who were visiting the Park. It was around mid-afternoon when the five of them started back down the trail together, in rather leisurely fashion. As it became steeper, they fell into single file, with Mazzer in the lead, followed by Nelson, Smitty and Nyhlen, with Brita bringing up the rear.

Grizzly Ahead

At 3:30 p.m., slightly more than a mile from the lake, they crossed an open meadow, spotted here and there with a few stunted firs. Ed Mazzer, still in the lead, started around a slight curve in the path at the forest's edge. Suddenly his heart jumped. Twenty-five yards ahead of him lumbered a huge female bear with two cubs, coming up the trail toward the hikers. In the same instant the grizzly lifted her head and froze, her tiny weak eyes trying to focus.

Mazzer turned and ran back up the trail toward his companions, shouting "Bear! Bear! Bear with cubs! Get up a tree! Get up a tree!" Nelson heard the warning and repeated it. The group scattered — Mazzer and the Swedish couple on one side of the trail, Nelson and Smitty on the other. As they did so, the huge animal continued up the trail, now running rapidly toward them.

Mazzer was the first to scramble up a tree, and Nyhlen did the same nearby. On the other side of the trail, Nelson and Smitty, running at top speed, headed for a clump of trees, the boy behind the ranger. The grizzly headed for the boy, and Smitty, glancing over his shoulder to find the bear almost on top of him, flopped face down on the ground to protect his vital parts and tried to cover his head with his arms. Lunging forward, the huge beast pounced upon him, growling, clawing, snarling and tossing him about.

Nelson turned sharply, just in time to see the bear start tearing skin off the back of Smitty's head. Then she turned him half over and raked her claws across his face; and finally, she picked him up and threw him so that he landed on his back. Nelson, now standing behind an old and rotten tree, began shouting to distract the animal.

"Stay On Your Stomach!"

The grizzly looked up, saw him, and charged. Frantically, Nelson tried to get up the tree. Branches broke as he tried to climb, and although he did get about four feet off the ground, the bear grabbed his buttocks with her teeth and pulled him down. Nelson hit the ground with a crash and somehow managed to get over on his face. He could hear Mazzer shouting "Stay on your stomach!"

The bear tore at him with teeth and claws, and seemed to be trying to turn him over on his back. Nelson felt that he had a better chance by playing dead, and the only fighting he did was to try to stay on his stomach. The bear bit him in the thighs several times and then suddenly stopped. Apparently she had heard the others climbing their trees. The animal wheeled and charged the Swedish couple.

Nyhlen had succeeded in climbing to a safe height, but Brita Noring was still on the ground when the beast reached her. Momentarily it was distracted by Mazzer in a nearby tree, who was yelling wildly and barking like a dog to draw the grizzly's attention. Brita Noring began to climb but could get no higher than a few feet. When the bear returned to her tree, it reared up, caught her in the thigh and dragged her down.

As she lay wounded on the ground, the grizzly stood growling, grunting and tearing at her. Seizing her by the thigh, it dragged her from one side of the tree to the other and several yards through the underbrush. Then, said Brita: "For a moment she left me, but she came back and gave me a bite in the left arm. I thought I was finished, but then she ran away."

The Grizzly Departs

Still panting and grunting, the grizzly ran from Miss Noring to Nelson and then to Smitty. All lay very still, pretending to be dead. Mazzer and Nyhlen were still safe in their trees. For several minutes the bear remained on the scene, not molesting anyone. Then she disappeared into the brush.

A deadly quiet descended upon the meadow, broken only by the distant murmur of the creek down in the gorge. No one dared move lest the huge beast be lurking nearby, ready to charge them again.

Ten minutes passed. Twenty minutes. At about 4:15 Mazzer and

Nyhlen climbed out of their trees, and went to Brita, Nelson and Smitty, checking their injuries. They found Smitty conscious but blood-soaked and unable to see. Obviously he was gravely wounded. Nelson was prostrate, his legs covered with blood. Brita lay where the grizzly had dropped her, bleeding but still conscious.

Mazzer knelt by Nelson and the two rangers held a hurried conference. They decided that both Mazzer and Nyhlen should go for help. If the bear attacked them on the trail, one man might get through. As for the bear's victims, all the two men could do was to try to make them comfortable and leave them as they were, on the ground.

Mazzer and Nyhlen started out, running at first, then proceeding more slowly in case the grizzly was still about. Now, for the injured, began the long ordeal of waiting. Despite the danger, they began calling quietly back and forth in their pain. Smitty's eyesight gone, he could not see the others; but he did not cry. Nelson knew that his injuries were severe and, because of the pain throbbing through his thighs, wondered if he would ever be able to walk again. The sun beating down on him became uncomfortable, and he painfully dragged himself to some nearby shade.

Blood Bath

Smitty, his face covered with blood, finally was able to open his right eye. Slowly, his face and body burning with agony, he pulled himself to his feet, took one unsteady step and fell on his face. Again he got up, and found he was in the middle of the trail. About ten yards away he saw Nelson lying in the grass and stumbled in his direction.

Nelson, racked by his own pain, was just rousing himself to call out again to the others when he heard what sounded like "very heavy footsteps." He jerked his head around to see Smitty lurching toward him, the boy's face, chest and body bloody and horribly mutilated. The ranger asked: "Smitty, can you see?"

"Yes, a little," came the answer. "But my arm is broken."

Nelson reached out and, touching him lightly, got the boy to lie down beside him. Opening his knapsack, he took out a shirt and sweatshirt. With them he covered the boy's chest, arms and face to keep off mosquitoes and to keep him warm. Smitty was shivering convulsively from shock. Using his arms, Nelson dragged himself toward Smitty and drew him closer.

Smitty grew terribly thirsty and asked for a drink of water. Nelson had none, and even if he had would not have given the boy any for fear of internal injuries. Smitty told Nelson how he had "played dead" after the first attack. Then he began to ask questions about the rescue party, about his own condition, and about the Swedish lady. Nelson tried to ease his mind as best he could.

Going For Help

At 6:05 p.m. Ed Mazzer and Gote Nyhlen descended the last steep grade of the Okotomi trail and emerged in the area of the Rising Sun Campground. They jumped into Mazzer's car and roared onto the Going-To-The-Sun Highway, heading for the ranger station at St. Mary, six miles away. At 6:15 the car skidded to a stop before the residence of District Ranger James Godboldt.

Godboldt rose to meet the two men on the porch and listened intently to Mazzer's story; then he ran to the radio room in the headquarters adjoining his residence. Rangers, fire guards and trail crewmen piled out of trailers, cabins and dormitories. Within minutes a nine-man crew was outfitted with standard stretchers and a special carrier equipped with two large, cycle-type wheels, first-aid blankets, a pack-set radio and two high-powered rifles. The crew left for the Rising Sun Campground at 6:30 p.m. and began the long ascent into the mountains, now darkening above them in the evening light.

One man was left at St. Mary as a communications anchor; another remained at Rising Sun to direct operations from a base camp there at the foot of the trail. A follow-up rescue crew was organized and Dr. Lewis Reese at Many Glacier Hotel, resident physician for the eastern side of the Park, was alerted. He hung up the phone, shouted the news to his wife, a registered nurse, and they headed with his medical equipment for Rising Sun by automobile.

At 7:00 p.m. a second rescue crew, consisting of 11 men, left Rising Sun, this group including Lloyd Parratt, Smitty's father. Twenty minutes later a third crew consisting of five rangers from the Many Glacier area set out from Rising Sun, carrying another stretcher and more emergency equipment. With this group was Smitty's 19-year-old brother Mark.

More Help Arrives

At 7:45 p.m. Dr. Reese and his wife drove into the campground. They at once set up an emergency first-aid station under lights the rangers had begun to string up under the trees. Picnic tables were covered with blankets, and blood plasma bottles were attached to poles. At the edge of the shadows stood three ranger ambulances. Godboldt kept track of things on a walkie-talkie that sputtered and crackled in the mountain night. The air was turning cold.

An advance party of three men from the first rescue party, carrying first-aid kits and a high-powered rifle, reached the scene of the attack about 7:45 p.m. They found all three victims conscious. No complaint came from Smitty, except that he was burning with thirst. Afraid to give him a proper drink, one of the men wet a clean handkerchief from his canteen of water and pressed it to the boy's lips.

At 8:00 p.m. the main body of the first rescue crew arrived. The first job was to bind up the more serious wounds in order to avoid major bleeding as the victims were carried down the rough trail on a stretcher. At 8:30 the second rescue party reached the meadow, now a weird scene of stabbing lights and dark figures; and before long the five-man party of rangers from Many Glacier emerged from the shadows of the trail. Smitty's father had come with the second group, his brother Mark with the Many Glacier group.

Down The Dark Trail

At 9:00 o'clock the boy, now carefully bandaged, was lifted onto a stretcher and the stretcher was placed upon a wheel carrier. Front and back, husky men held the stretcher as it bumped on its big wheels down the steep and rocky trail. Others in the party kept their lights focused on the path. Guards with rifles at the ready moved in front and brought up the rear. One ranger stayed beside Smitty, keeping a constant check on his condition.

At 9:15 Brita Noring was lifted onto a stretcher and her two-hour descent began. Nelson was started down a few minutes later. A small army was required to service the entire operation, some 37 men in all.

Finally, at 10:45, the party with Smitty arrived at the foot of the trail. The boy was still conscious and able to talk briefly. Dr. Reese splinted Smitty's arm and placed it in a sling, then cleansed all wounds as much as possible. He bandaged the boy's torn head and started feeding a saline solution through his veins. A ranger ambulance was backed up to the area and Smitty was lifted into its rear while a ranger climbed in to hold the bottle containing the saline solution. Two visiting tourists with compatible Type O blood also got in, having volunteered to furnish transfusions, if needed.

Forty-two miles to the north, the hospital at Cardston, Alberta, had been alerted to get ready for the emergency. Two extra physicians had been summoned from Lethbridge, 57 miles away. Customs officials at the Canadian border had been alerted and opened the gates that were ordinarily closed at that hour. At 11:55 Smitty arrived at Cardston Municipal Hospital and was wheeled into the emergency room. Two minutes later, two precious pints of whole blood arrived from Lethbridge.

The Doctors Take Over

At 12:20 a.m. Brita Noring arrived at the hospital and at 1:45 the ambulance bearing Nelson reached the hospital. Nelson was conscious but in extreme pain with deeper wounds than the others.

From midnight on, three and sometimes four doctors — with nurses and attendants — worked for a solid nine-and-one-half hours to complete surgery on the three victims. Brita Noring was found to have extensive lacerations of the right leg with severe muscle damage and loss of skin, severe lacerations to the right buttock, and puncture wounds in the right shoulder. Alan Nelson had severe lacerations on the back of both thighs and his right knee, with considerable muscle damage to his left upper leg. The condition of both was considered satisfactory.

Smitty Parratt had puncture wounds in his right chest, a collapsed right lung, two fractures apiece for each of five ribs, a compound fracture of the right upper arm, extensive scalp lacerations, extreme damage to the eye area of his face, loss of his left eye and a compound fracture of facial bones. His condition was regarded as critical. His parents were told that it was doubtful if he would survive and, if he did, he would be blind the rest of his life.

The boy suffered excruciating pain. Infection brought on fever.

Only a sunken socket remained of his left eye, and his right eye, when the bandages were removed, was so swollen that months would pass before partial vision returned. And yet, amazingly, he continued to live. Finally, after long weeks his condition began to improve.

The Injured Go Home

In the meantime, the Swedish vice-consul from Calgary, Alberta had driven Brita Noring from the hospital to Calgary in late July. She was placed on a plane to New York, and then flew on to Stockholm, her wounds healing without complications. Shortly thereafter, Alan Nelson was back home in Bismarck, North Dakota, well on the road to recovery.

But for Smitty Parratt, a pattern of many operations lay ahead. Several months of healing were required between each operation. The surgery was begun as soon as the immediate threat to his life had passed. In mid-August, he was flown to Los Angeles for specialized treatment at Children's Hospital where the first operation took place on September 8th. This was plastic surgery, designed to improve a shortening of the optic nerve and muscles of the right eye. It now appeared there would be vision in the eye when the swelling had receded.

It was not until November 1st that the plastic surgeon, Dr. James Johnson, operated to remove dead bone from Smitty's right cheek. On April 18, 1961, he worked to remove and reduce scars in this area. On September 5, 1961, he began a series of operations to reduce several large scars on the back of the head. On January 9, 1962, he performed a skin graft under Smitty's right eye. On May 17th, he completed the skin graft on the right cheek.

Then, in the late summer of 1962, the injuries to Smitty's ribs brought on osteomyelitis, and in October he underwent his eighth operation at Children's hospital. Portions of two ribs were removed, but he rallied amazingly from this unexpected setback.

Unending Surgery

The surgeons turned once more to the scars on the boy's head, but Dr. Johnson's best efforts were unsuccessful. This was a particularly

114

dark period for Smitty. He was in much pain, had to wear large head bandages, and was out of school for weeks at a time. His twelfth operation took place on June 11, 1964, the last performed by the family's beloved Dr. Johnson, who died three months later of a heart attack.

Fortunately, an able successor was found in the person of Dr. Wilmer C. Hansen, a tall, warm-hearted plastic surgeon who responded with instant sympathy for Smitty's problems. In December, 1964, he performed surgery to reconstruct Smitty's left tear duct. In April, 1965, he set out to reconstruct the right tear duct (the good eye), but discovered that the area had been too badly shattered. Instead he removed bone fragments to advance the right medial canthus (the inside corner or fold of the eye), which had been displaced by the crushed bone.

Six weeks later, he went to work on the large stubborn scar on the back of Smitty's head. This time surgery was followed by X-ray treatments. Further operations were planned to complete the work on the head scar, to reconstruct a bridge for the nose, and to reattach the inside corner of each of the eyes to either side of the nose.

The cost of all this treatment was enormous. In recognition of the family's plight, Congress enacted a special statutory act (H.R. 4141, dated December 21, 1963), giving the Parratts the privilege of bringing suit against the government although the two-year statute of limitations had expired. (A previous suit brought by the victim of another grizzly attack in Glacier Park had resulted in a $100,000 judgment for the victim in 1961). As the result of this congressional action, the Parratts were able to negotiate a satisfactory settlement with the government.

How has Smitty's long-drawn-out ordeal affected him? As he phrased it:

> At first I was just nothing. I'd lie around the house after the operations. We had this little TV set at home. When I was back in school, I only made B's and C's.

Turning Point

In time, however, his grades improved. He began to participate again in outside activities. He joined the Explorer Scouts and there had the strengthening experience of being accepted by other boys with no special privileges and no comments on his appearance. Barred from contact sports by his injuries, he went out for track and won two letters, one in the 660-yard run. He played the saxophone in his school band, and although he found marching difficult because of his limited peripheral vision, he was chosen the best freshman in the band. On the basis of these achievements and his straight-A grades, the faculty selected him from a class of 400 as the outstanding freshman of the year.

Smitty came to feel that life had almost returned to normal, saying:

> I don't think about it until people stare at my face — then I remember it. This is the hardest part, people staring at me and asking questions.

He dreaded the operations, but felt that he must continue to endure them because he knew they would help and because he could see the improvement himself.

Smitty's love of nature has remained as strong as ever, and especially his love for Glacier National Park. First taken there as a baby of seven months, he continued to return with his family every summer, even after the accident. Finally, however, came a summer when he had to remain in California; and it saddened him that for the first time in his life he was not able to spend the summer in the great park.

XIII

THE TWIN TRAGEDIES OF 1967

Not since the sinking of the Titanic have America's newspaper readers recoiled with such horror as on August 14, 1967, when they were greeted by reports of the savage mangling and killing of two lovely young women by enraged grizzly bears in the mountains of Glacier National Park. For a time, such headlines as "Night of Terror" and "Grizzlies Kill Girls" shoved war stories, race riots and traffic deaths off the main line of the news.

Hardly had the recounting of full particulars of the gruesome tale subsided when throughout the press and leading magazines of the country, as well as among the citizenry generally, a tremendous controversy began to rage over the question of whether grizzlies and humans should continue to co-exist in the national parks. The Park Service was besieged with heavy criticism, as well as a large amount of unsolicited advice, as to what it should have done, and ought to be doing about the situation. Every bear expert in the country, from Andy Russell to Gairdner Moment, broke into print on the subject, adding his particular fuel to the flames.

Not only was there intense distress and revulsion over the fact that two attractive young women had become victims of the mightiest beast in the national parks, but there was vast puzzlement among experts and tyros alike over the question of why, after nearly sixty years of freedom from lethal encounters with *Ursus horribilis* in Glacier Park, tragedy should strike twice on the same August night in different locations, both victims being park employees, both female and 19, and both being attacked while in sleeping bags at a campground with others under circumstances involving no provocation by those attacked or their companions.

The story giving rise to the headlines of August, 1967 has been told and re-told a number of times. The action took place in two areas of Glacier, both on the western side of the Continental Divide, but several miles apart. Granite Park is a mountain chalet situated at an elevation of about 6500 feet near Swiftcurrent Pass, while Trout Lake, at an elevation of 3880 feet, lies approximately seven miles northwest of Lake McDonald.

Tragedy Number One

Among those arriving at Granite Park on the late afternoon of Saturday, August 12, 1967, were Roy Ducat and Julie Helgesen, both employed at the lodge at East Glacier, she in the laundry, he as a busboy. His home was at Perrysburg, Ohio, and although only 18, he was already a sophomore at Bowling Green University, majoring in biology. Julie was 19, a native of Albert Lea, Minnesota, and prominent in school activities while in high school. She was now a sophomore at the University of Minnesota.

Julie and Roy had been at East Glacier for nearly two months when they had opportunity for a special week-end holiday. Packing their gear, including lunches from the lodge kitchen, they hitch-hiked to Logan Pass, then hiked eight miles of Garden Wall trail to Granite Park. They arrived at about seven o'clock, but it was nearly eight before they finally decided to spend the night at the official campground, where there were a few other sojourners. They had been warned of the danger of bears, but laughed and said they were not afraid. After all, no one had ever been killed by a bear in Glacier Park. Nevertheless, Roy carefully buried the remnants of their meal a few hundred feet away. Then they got into their sleeping bags and soon fell asleep.

About 12:45 a.m. the pair was awakened by an investigative bear which savagely attacked both of them, then carried Julie screaming into the darkness. Despite the severity of his wounds, Roy managed to arouse others in the campground area, and word of the attack was relayed to the Chalet several hundred yards up the trail. When the impact of the message was realized, a search party was formed and warily proceeded with flashlights to the campground.

Rescue Operation

There they found Roy Ducat in a semi-conscious condition and bleeding heavily from his wounds. After he was given first aid, members of the party carried him up the trail to the Chalet, while Ranger-Naturalist Joan Devereaux (now Joan Watson, having married Ranger Tom Watson in 1971) succeeded in contacting Park Fire Headquarters by two-way radio, advising them of the attack, and requesting aid and medical supplies. Headquarters responded that a helicopter would arrive in twenty or thirty minutes with supplies and an armed ranger. When it arrived, Roy Ducat was loaded and flown to the hospital at Kalispell, where he underwent surgery for three hours.

Ranger Gary Bunney, armed with a heavy-duty Winchester, and several volunteers set out in the three a.m. darkness for the campground. On reaching the site, they cautiously fanned out in several directions, since they had no means of knowing which way the grizzly had made off with Julie. Finally, to the left and down the slope, they heard a faint cry and hastened in its direction. They came upon the girl lying on her face, covered with blood and barely alive. Gently they gave her first aid, and by means of an improvised stretcher got her back to the Chalet and onto an improvised operating table where she was ministered to by three physicians who happened to be guests at the Chalet. It was 4 a.m. when another guest, Father Connolly, baptized her, gave her absolution for her sins, and she breathed her last. In a few moments, the helicopter was on its way with her body, winging through the darkness to Kalispell.

Nightly Show At Granite Park

What Julie Helgesen and Roy Ducat did not know, not that it would necessarily have affected their course of action, was that the vicinity of Granite Park was a grizzly bear hangout; that regularly each evening around dusk, two or more grizzlies would appear in the gully at the rear of the Chalet where its garbage was dumped, and feed there for half an hour or longer; that this had become a "showtime" for Chalet guests and on a few occasions for some of the Park's Rangers and Ranger-Naturalists. Nor had they heard of the old sow with two cubs that had sometimes been seen about the

119

garbage dump after other bears had departed, or that their tracks had been noted, especially in the mornings, in the same vicinity.

Early in August, spectators at the regular evening performance had included a ranger-naturalist, his wife, and two members of the Park Headquarters staff at West Glacier. They heard reports that grizzlies were making nightly appearances at the Chalet and decided to hike up after work and see for themselves. When they arrived at Granite Park, they were told that two bears had been showing up each evening, and that the tracks of another adult bear with cubs were often seen in the vicinity of the dump in the morning. They were rewarded by seeing the two regulars approach the garbage pit around ten p.m. and eat their fill. As they were leaving around midnight for the return hike, they were attracted by noises in the vicinity of the dump, and upon investigation, found it occupied by a large grizzly and her two cubs, busily feeding on the leftovers. They then hastened back to West Glacier, feeling rather fortunate to have seen, not one or two, but five of the great animals in the course of a single brief visit.

Tragedy Number Two

The helicopter with Julie's body had hardly taken off from Granite Park when the scene of action shifted to the Trout Lake area, some ten miles west of Granite Park. Five young Park concessioner employees had hiked in with overnight gear, intending to spend the night. The group consisted of three young men and two girls.

Two of the boys were brothers, Ron and Ray Noseck, from Oracle, Arizona. Ray, 23, was a dental student at the University of Louisville and, in the summer season, manager of a service station near Lake McDonald Lodge. His brother Ron, 21, also a dental student at Louisville, was employed as a waiter at the Lodge at East Glacier. Their dates for the trip were Denise Huckle, 20, a room clerk at East Glacier, and Michele Koons, 19, employed at the gift shop at Lake McDonald Lodge. Both girls were college students, Michele a sophomore at California Western University near her home in San Diego. The fifth member of the party was 16-year-old Paul Dunn, of Edina, Minnesota, who had accepted a job as a busboy at East Glacier Lodge, in the course of a visit to the Park with his parents. He had been invited along on the trip by his fellow-employee at East Glacier, Ron Noseck.

With them on the trail across the slopes of Mt. Stanton was Squirt, an abandoned puppy that had been befriended by Denise and brought along on the trip, strictly against Park regulations. They had crossed a little plateau, after climbing nearly 2000 feet, and hiked down the trail toward Trout Lake. They had originally planned to continue another two miles to Arrow Lake, but decided against it when they encountered a couple of fishermen who told how they had been treed in that area by a troublesome bear. However, this news did not particularly dampen their ardor. Getting run up a tree was part of the fun and adventure of Glacier Park, and they knew that no one had ever been killed by a bear in the Park.

The Camp At Trout Lake

They set up camp on the shore of Trout Lake, near the logjam at its end. Michele remained in camp with the dog while the others fished until eight o'clock. Then, while they were cooking hot dogs around the campfire, Michele spotted a bear in nearby trees. They hastily retreated down the shore some fifty yards, as a scrawny brown grizzly invaded their camp, appropriating their food, strolling leisurely from dish to dish before taking its departure.

When they were able to return to camp, the terrified youngsters found practically all their food had been eaten. They considered returning to Lake McDonald, but were deterred by the inky darkness and the fact that they had only one flashlight. They decided instead to move camp to another location farther along the shore. There they gathered old logs and built a cheerful fire which they determined to keep burning throughout the night. They arranged their sleeping bags in a semi-circle around the fire and fell into a nervous slumber.

Grizzly Invasion

Well after midnight they were awakened by disturbing sounds that caused them to rebuild the fire to a more reassuring level. At times the sound seemed to come from shallow water below the camp, and again from the woods above. They placed a sack of cookies overlooked by bruin in the earlier foray on the edge of a log, from which it disappeared in a few minutes. At 4:30 a.m., when the fire had died down again, the camp was suddenly invaded by a bear that began sniffing at the sleeping bags. Paul Dunn leaped out of his, and hastily climbed a nearby tree from which he was able, by the dim light of the campfire, to survey the scene below.

The camp was now in a frenzy as the others tried to escape the marauder. Ron Noseck helped Denise into a tree and threw the dog up to her. Ray played dead in his sleeping bag as the bear sniffed at him and moved on; then rolled out of the bag and raced to a tree, calling to Michele to do the same. When the zipper to her bag became stuck, the bear began tearing at her arm. As the others watched helplessly, the bear dragged her into the woods, sleeping bag and all, and they heard her scream, "Oh, my God, I'm dead."

At dawn, the four survivors climbed down from their trees and wearily stumbled back over the trail toward Lake McDonald and the ranger cabin near its north end. A ranger-led rescue party, including Ron Noseck and Paul Dunn, rushed back to Trout Lake. There, at the end of a trail of blood, bits of sleeping bag and clothing, they found Michele's badly mangled body, not much over 100 feet from the camp.

Four Questions Posed By The Twin Attacks

Both before and after these incidents there had been other grizzly attacks in Glacier, which it would serve no purpose to describe. Except for the 1967 incidents, none had a fatal ending, and none had involved a raid by a grizzly bear, definitely identified as such, upon a camp site, campground or sleeping bag occupant. With one exception, no attack had ever been made on a ranger-guided party or caused wounds of great severity. Nearly all the attacks were unprovoked and most were perpetrated by a mother grizzly with cubs.

With an increase in the number of Park visitors through the years, and a correspondingly greater frequency of ursine encounters, there came also a greater appreciation of the dangers involved. Particularly was it realized that a primary part of the problem lay in the failure to perceive that with bears, as with humans, familiarity breeds contempt; and that such contempt was being engendered by the feeding of the great quadrupeds, and by their resultant familiarization with human beings, human locales, and human food. Early steps were taken to minimize the contacts by the elimination of hotel garbage dumps, by prohibiting the feeding of bears by visitors, and by the removal of so-called "bum bears" from scenes of their begging to remote wilderness areas of the Park.

No intensive studies of the bear problem were made, however, and by 1957 the annual visitor volume to Glacier had reached 700,000; by 1967, it was hovering around the million mark. Thousands of visitors were flooding the trails and marching through wilderness backcountry, bringing human food and distributing human garbage wherever they went. The enforcement of rules designed to minimize the bear hazard became more difficult and, at some locations at least, providing garbage feasts for neighboring bears was still passively tolerated.

When the twin tragedies of August 13, 1967 burst on a stunned world, including Park officialdom, it triggered a massive reaction, and a review of measures that could and should be taken to insure against recurrence of such fatalities, and that bear encounters would be reduced to a minimum. As a result of the hue and cry, the situation received a thorough airing, making it evident that there were at least four questions for which answers were sorely needed.

Related Or Unrelated?

Could it be that two grizzly attacks in the same national park on the same night, both on 19-year-old girls in sleeping bags, both unprovoked and both fatal, were matters of mere coincidence? Although not the most important of the four questions, this is certainly the most perplexing and intriguing. Never in the history of Glacier had any life heretofore been sacrificed, nor apparently had it been seriously considered that any would be. To be asked to believe the two events were totally unrelated boggles the mind.

At first some consideration had been directed toward the question of whether the situation involved one bear or two; but this was quickly resolved when the geography was examined and it was realized that the two attack sites, though separated by only nine airline miles, were thirty trail miles apart, with an 8,000-foot mountain range in between. But if two bears were involved, what could have been the coordinating factor, if such there was? Why the same night, and not too far from the same hour? Why, indeed, after 57 years of co-existence unmarked by any fatality and with relatively few attacks, should there happen, almost simultaneously, not one, but two deaths? What might the odds be against occurrence of such a double tragedy?

When statistics became available, they only served to intensify the mystery and more definitely to point the finger at eerie coincidence. On the basis of computerized calculations, the odds against one such killing on a given night were reported to be 1,000,000 to 1 with the odds against two the same night rocketing to 1,000,000,000,000 to 1. Of course, what comes out of a computer depends entirely upon input, which in this case would have to include a base figure of zero deaths in Glacier for the first 57 years of its existence.

Astronomical Odds

But other statistics produce the same result. During the 1960's the average of five bear injuries per year in all national parks inhabited by such animals represented one injury for each 1,500,000 visitors, or 0.007 per cent. Another approach would be to compare the number of bear-induced fatalities in Glacier for the decade of the 1960's with its visitor-volume for the same period, and this would produce odds of approximately 4,175,000 to 1, or 0.0024 per cent. Whatever the statistical method used, it provides no answer to our question.

While some experts have simply declined to accept such an explanation as reasonable, Andy Russell, an acknowledged expert on the grizzly and its behavior, said that he was as sure as any man could be that the happenings of August 13, 1967 represented nothing more than sheer coincidence. This was also the opinion of most of those qualified to express one, including Ruben Hart, then Chief Ranger at Glacier.

It is believed by some that the simultaneity of the two incidents can be understood only through a recognition that man and grizzly have been on a collision course from the time they first came in contact with each other on the North American continent, that by 1967 man with his offensive smell and antagonistic ways has been pushing the grizzly farther and farther back into his limited space, and that conditions of that summer at certain places in the Park made an explosion of the growing tension inevitable. While this theory is a plausible one, even its proponents concede it was pure coincidence that two grizzlies chose a few hours of a single night to strike two victims who had so much in common.

Cause Or Causes Of The Attacks?

Whether or not the events of the night of August 13, 1967 were purely coincidental in character, what were the reasons that brought about their occurrence? At the outset this, too, seemed to be a question for which there was no very good answer, and many theories were tentatively advanced with a view to explaining why two bears, as if on a prearranged signal, killed two girls. Those considering the matter took note, of course, of the fact that both guilty animals were females, and that the one at Granite Park had cubs, often a circumstance connected with such attacks. But even though the female is more deadly than the male, bears with cubs had never previously taken human life in Glacier, and the bear at Trout Lake *had no cubs.*

Rabies as a possible cause was ruled out in both cases by official tests made on the bodies of the offending bears which, of course, had been promptly slain after the attacks. The factor of weather was suggested, since it had been a season of unusually high temperatures, of thunder, lightning and raging forest fires; and other animals have been known to become restless under the influence of such phenomena. Potential aggravation from these sources was negatived, however, by opinions on grizzly behavior and reactions. Such things as cosmetics and perfume were suspected, since the victims were young and feminine; and even the possibility of female odors was cited, since one of the girls was known to have been menstruating at the time, and the other apparently about to.

One rather unusual theory was predicated on the fact that both girls had been dragged away from their camp sites in their sleeping bags. It was hypothesized by two of Glacier's top naturalists that since bears have been learning to open packaged food perhaps they thought the sleeping bags were packages; that possibly sleeping bags themselves might worry a bear, or it might become alarmed

125

upon finding a strange cocoon with something warm and alive inside. Not enough is really known about grizzly behavior to rule out any of these ingenious theories completely, but the fact remains that, without any of them, there is a simple and sufficient answer to the question of causation in each of these cases.

Midnight Visitors

In reference to the Granite Park attack, the evidence indicated two very pertinent causative factors. To begin with, the killer bear was a female with cubs and the responsibility for keeping them fed. More importantly, however, the chalet personnel had followed a nightly pattern of dumping garbage in the gully some 50 yards behind the chalet, where grizzlies would come at a regular hour each evening to feast, usually with an audience of spellbound humans only yards away. The old female and her cubs did not ordinarily appear until around midnight; nevertheless, she had been seen there and undoubtedly had become accustomed to human surroundings, odors, and food, and possibly had come to rely upon the latter as a source of sustenance.

This was the unhappy background of her August 13th behavior. Who knows but that the garbage on that night, and perhaps for two or three previous nights, had been so thoroughly picked over by earlier foragers as to leave little or nothing for the old female, thus driving her to seek other sources of food for herself and cubs, or perhaps enraging her to the point where she became sufficiently irrational to put aside her normal fear of man? The whole picture was in violation of the most basic rule of bear management: the rule against feeding bears or providing them with inducements to hang around areas inhabited or frequented by humans.

Activities Of The Rogue Bear

As to the Trout Lake attack, the evidence is different but equally clear. It had been a long, hot summer, and the berry crop on which bears depend for food was rather scant. All season long a skinny, odd-shaped female grizzly had been haunting the area of Arrow Lake and Trout Lake. As far back as the latter part of June, this animal had been raiding camps of visitors to the sector, opening cans of food, ripping into packs and first-aid kits, and destroying other gear. For the next several weeks, it not only continued these tactics, but began to harass hikers to and from Lake McDonald, following a few yards behind for considerable distances and frightening them. The bear's strange behavior was repeatedly reported to Park authorities.

This bizarre animal not only invaded camps with great regularity, but refused to be scared away by yelling or stone throwing. It methodically slashed packs into small pieces, bent the frames, and gobbled up any available food. The report of an encounter between two Columbia Falls youths and this skinny brown grizzly even appeared in the *Hungry Horse News* for August 4, 1967. When the camp of a girl scout troop from Kalispell was invaded by the same bear, destroying their food and belongings, they fled the scene. However, one of the girls paused long enough to take a picture of the rogue bear, a picture which appeared on the front page of the *Daily Inter Lake,* Kalispell's newspaper, on Thursday, August 10, 1967. By this time, its operations in the Trout Lake area had become a matter of general information.

When, later on, the nefarious activities of the Trout Lake bear were skillfully pieced together by a master reporter, it became apparent not only that she had been waging a campaign of guerrilla warfare against campers in the area for nearly two months prior to the events of August 13th, but that she had grown bolder with each passing week. The only wonder was that her persistent hit-run tactics had not sooner culminated in tragedy.

The Grizzlies Must Go: The Anti-Grizzly View

In the light of tragic experience in Glacier and Yellowstone, is it advisable for bears and people to co-exist in the national parks? There is a considerable body of informed opinion holding that such co-existence is not practicable. No one has gone so far as to urge the outright extinction of the park grizzlies, but they have taken the position that these great quadrupeds are exceedingly dangerous animals, the most dangerous, in fact, on the North American continent; that as such, they should be excluded from national parks and be permitted to continue their existence only in wilderness areas unfrequented by man, such as parts of Alaska and northwest Canada. One eminent biologist feels that the Park Service should make up its mind whether it wants to run a park for people or for bears, and if it seems important to conserve the grizzly, there are other suitable habitats.

Those who share this view feel that the danger to humans from a status of co-existence is too great, and that sooner or later the 1967 tragedies will be repeated with increasing frequency. These individuals hold that while, statistically, the number of people injured or killed by bears is small, this is not a valid reason for permitting the continuance of a dangerous condition. They suggest that while very few people have ever been injured or killed by falling from the top of the Washington Monument, this fact did not deter the National Park Service from putting up a protective guardrail.

Others point out that space is one of the prime needs of a grizzly, and that the "lower 48" states no longer have the space he requires; that if he is denied running room, and humans continue to come into ever-increasing contact with him, the grizzly will inevitably maim and kill. They assert that no matter what steps Park authorities take to improve the conditions for co-existence, a few summers may pass without serious injury, but sooner or later standards will slip, complacency will develop, and human error will recur. Then along will come another peculiar grizzly, like the one at Trout Lake, or one that has become dependent upon people-provided food, like the one at Granite Park, and "more human life will be sacrificed, almost as certainly as tamaracks lose their needles and beavers eat aspen bark."

The Grizzlies Should Stay: The Pro-Grizzly View

"Should the huge bears be allowed to roam free in U.S. national parks or should they be resettled in government-owned wilderness inaccessible to the public?" This was the sixty-four dollar question phrased by Science Digest Magazine in its October, 1969 article, the opening line of which began "The great grizzly controversy roars on." From a review of publications on the subject, it is apparent that the pro-grizzly faction outnumbers the antis considerably, the results running about three in favor of the bears to one against. An attitude survey of public opinion, conducted within a year or two following the Glacier Park fatalities, on the question of whether grizzlies should be eliminated from the national parks, showed only

104 out of 3,420 responses supporting such action, or less than 3%. What the public did favor was more effective management of people, bears and garbage.

The National Parks Magazine editorialized that "Hard as it may go against man's more selfish instincts, the grizzly has a right to the fragment of existence left to it. The future will not thank us should we commit genocide on such an animal." Another writer opined that "To destroy all bears would be unthinkable. But with campers flooding our woods, we must learn how to live with the animals whose land we invade."

Preservation Of The Grizzlies

Eldon G. Bowman, formerly a seasonal ranger in Glacier park, has stated that on the basis of his experience over several summers of field work, "people and bears can use the same area with risks reduced to an acceptable minimum. We have come full circle back to what the public wants and expects in regard to the parks, the wilderness and grizzlies. These big bears can and should be preserved in their natural settings, available for those who will make the effort and run the risks inherent in the wilderness to see them."

Other writers have indicated their preference for retention of the grizzly provided certain steps be taken to insure visitor safety. David Niven, for example, suggests that wilderness areas should be limited to day use with the possible exception of people who walk or take pack horses on back country trails. He adds: "There should be more roads and people should be required to view the animals from their cars" as is done "in the great parks of Africa, where parkland is considered the home of the animals which the people visit."

Andy Russell asserts that "summer hikers and campers using our national parks and wilderness country can travel the trails in grizzly country with almost complete safety. To those who might say that is not enough, I would reply that complete safety is not found anywhere in a man's life." He makes it clear, however, that such a statement presupposes that steps will be taken to provide for disposal of all park garbage through universal use of adequate incinerators, to institute firm enforcement of the regulations forbidding the feeding of bears within the parks, and to bring about thorough indoctrination of all hikers, campers and wilderness travelers in respect to the big bears, their habits and reactions.

Jean George concluded that "In the final analysis, it appears that man and grizzly can co-exist in our wilderness parks — but co-existence raises problems similar to those of managing traffic: it means more regulation and less freedom, to achieve greater safety. It also means enforcement of all regulations by the National Park Service."

A similar conclusion was reached by Roger Caras who insisted that the bear danger in Glacier had been over-dramatized by the wide-spread publicity accorded the events of August 13, 1967, and the correspondingly emotional over-reaction which followed on the part of many. In an effort to place the matter in proper perspective, he commented that "In truth, bear watching in an area administered by our National Park Service is one of the safest things a person can possibly find to do on a vacation. Flying, diving, swimming, boating, baseball, football, home carpentry and taking a shower are all more dangerous."

Magnificent Menace Or Natural Resource?

What do grizzly bears mean in a wilderness park? And what would be lost if these big bears were to disappear from our parks? For one thing, the grizzly is part and parcel of the wilderness ecosystem, with a vital place in the delicate balance of plant and animal life. Like many predators, he feeds on the weak and the sick, culling the unfit. He helps to regulate the numbers of small rodents which have a habit of over-populating their habitat and damaging the vegetation on which other forms of life are dependent.

Additionally, it should be recognized that the grizzly is as much a wonder of our land as the Grand Canyon or Old Faithful. Of himself, he is a unique natural resource — a magnificent, ferocious, unpredictable beast with a rare power to kindle the imagination and quicken the pulse. His is a dignity and power matched by no other on the North American continent. For many, the opportunity to share a mountain with him for a while is a privilege and an adventure like no other.

Finally, not the least of the values added by the grizzly to a wilderness park is verisimilitude. Wilderness means challenge, self-reliance and risk; it must include significant elements of all of these or it has no excuse for being set aside and preserved. The big bears represent an inherent part of that wilderness and of the risks which it includes. They are a symbolic, as well as an actual sign that there is still some authentic wilderness left.

Betsy Graff

A keen sense of smell aids the foraging grizzly.

Release of grizzly after its relocation by the National Park Service.

XIV

THE PARK SERVICE GRIZZLY PROGRAM

Many and varied are the responsibilities of the National Park Service in its role as manager and guardian of the nation's playgrounds and reservations. In two of the larger areas — Glacier and Yellowstone Parks — those responsibilities have been substantially increased by the presence of an extraordinary animal — the grizzly bear.

The powers of the Park Service, as well as its responsibilities, have had their inception, of course, in the 1916 Act of Congress which, in establishing the Service, defined its function as being "to conserve the scenery and the natural and historic objects and the wildlife therein and to provide for the enjoyment of the same in such manner and by such means as shall leave them unimpaired for the enjoyment of future generations." That the language in question may have contained something of an inherent conflict probably did not occur to anyone in 1916.

The Nature Of The Conflict

In attempting to conform to this general statement of policy, the Park Service has found itself not infrequently beset by two opposing points of view. On the one hand are the preservation-minded people who have felt that the words "conserve" and "unimpaired" should be taken literally, and that national parks should be maintained, as nearly as possible, in their original or natural state. These are folks who feel that the grizzly bear was part of the original scheme of things in Glacier and never should its status be changed.

Opposed to this viewpoint are those who have taken the position, and with great sincerity, that the language of the creational act required the national parks to be operated in such a manner and by such means as would best serve their enjoyment by the people; that if any feature of a park were to detract from or interfere with that enjoyment, steps should be taken to correct it. In short, if the grizzly begins to behave itself in such a manner as to endanger the life, health or safety of any member of present or future generations, it should be eliminated by one means or another.

Background Information

It has been the unhappy responsibility of the Park Service to reconcile, or attempt to resolve, the difference between the two factions, and to do so in conformity with the language of the founding Act. After all, the grizzly is a great natural resource, albeit a problem of substantial dimensions. Seemingly, it has turned out to be a problem that has only a 99.99% solution — a result that is not acceptable to those who have suffered mayhem or death by the paws or jaws of the big bears.

Park records indicate that the problem has not always been quite as serious as in recent years. For the first 46 years of Park history, i.e., from 1910 to 1956, injuries inflicted by grizzlies were minimal in number, and there were no fatalities. The picture began to change with the decade ending in 1966, during which there were 10 injuries, due perhaps to concurrent increases in grizzly population and the number of Park visitors. Most of these 10 incidents involved female grizzlies with cubs. Single adolescent and adult bears appeared to avoid direct conflicts with humans.

Beginning with 1966, the number of visitors to Glacier Park began to increase markedly, with visitations for the period 1966-1970 averaging over a million per year. Backcountry and trail activity grew out of all proportion to the general increase in visitors, and by 1970 backcountry travelers comprised approximately 5% to 10% of all visitors.

Need For Development Of A Program

In spite of the great increase in Park travel, there were only three confrontations with grizzlies during the five years ending with 1970, resulting in injuries to four people, but unfortunately two of these proved fatal, as reported in detail in an earlier chapter. The resulting shock to Park Service authorities, as well as to the country at large, led almost immediately to the decision that something would have to be done about the situation, and without delay.

It was this fateful decision which brought about the establishment in 1967 of an Office of Natural Science Studies for Glacier National Park, located at Park headquarters near West Glacier. To man this office, the Park Service employed Clifford J. Martinka, a research biologist whose educational background included degrees in zoology and wildlife management at Montana State University, Bozeman, Montana. Since 1967, Martinka has conducted ecological studies of grizzly bears and wintering ungulates and, so far as expertise in the field of the grizzly and its behavior is concerned, he is undoubtedly among the top half-dozen in the country, along with the Craighead brothers, G.F. Cole and Larry Roop, all of whom have become familiar with the grizzly in its Yellowstone habitat.

Following the institution of new measures based upon the Martinka studies, the record seemed to improve. Despite 15 confrontations or incidents during the period 1968-1972, there was but one injury. In 1972, the final year of that period, there were seven belligerent incidents involving equipment damage in five of them, but still no injuries. As the number of Park visitors mounted rapidly in the next four years, the situation rocked along until the season of 1976, when there were a total of 24 confrontations, resulting in 4 injuries, one of which proved fatal.

A Difference In 1976 Confrontations

The unprovoked and fatal assault upon a 1976 visitor not only came as a severe shock to all concerned, but also raised grave questions as to how it could have happened and how it could have been prevented. In this connection, an analysis of statistics for the season of 1976 has disclosed two new and puzzling facets of the grizzly problem: (1) The kind of grizzlies that were responsible for

135

most of the confrontations and all of the injuries; and (2) the locations where some of these confrontations took place.

Prior to 1976, a high percentage of Glacier Park injuries had been inflicted by mother bears with cubs, or by adult bears taken by surprise. In 1976, most of the incidents, including all of those causing injuries, involved adolescent, or subadult, animals, i.e., two or three-year-olds just turned loose by their mothers and apparently in search of a home range for themselves.

Finding its own home range becomes a problem for every young bear that must strike out for itself in an area where the density of occupancy by older bears has left no room for adolescent expansion. The desperation of his plight at such a time may overcome his natural inhibitions, in this case, his desire to avoid man, and lead him into a life of crime, i.e., into taking actions which would be entirely foreign to members of the species under ordinary circumstances.

Campground Invasions

The second new and startling development of 1976 was the place or places of confrontation. Three of the incidents took place in camps, two of them established campgrounds in developed areas. In previous years, with the exception of the two 1967 fatalities, invasions of camp sites were practically unknown, and belligerent visits to established campgrounds by grizzlies were simply unheard of. Statistics compiled by Martinka for the years 1968-1972 indicate that roughly 80% of the incidents during those years occurred in backcountry areas, and that the grizzly rarely became a nuisance in the vicinity of developed areas.

The Glacier Park authorities have made strenuous efforts to ascertain the grizzly population of the Park, and incidentally to obtain data concerning the status, dynamics and habitat relationships of the big bears. Studies were made during the period 1967-1971 in a sample area of the Park with the thought that a projection of the number of animals therein could serve as a basis for estimating the total grizzly population. A figure of 194 bears for the Park as a whole was arrived at (a mean for the 5-year period) although a high of 230 was obtained for the year 1969. This provided no indication, of course, as to whether some valleys or other areas might be overcrowded, i.e., beyond their habitat carrying capacity, while others remain underpopulated.

Affirmative Program

The Park Service has adopted a variety of measures designed to make the Park safe for its more than a million and a half visitors per annum. The program may be outlined as follows:

(1) Adoption of an expanded public relations program for hikers and other visitors.

(a) Weekly lectures on the grizzly by naturalists at key points in the Park.

(b) Publication of detailed information concerning the big bears.

(c) Distribution of strong warnings to visitors against having anything in camp or on the trail that will attract a hungry bear; and against doing anything of an antagonistic or bear-baiting character.

(d) Issuance of instructions to backcountry users with respect to the Park's "Pack-in, Pack-out" policy on litter.

(2) Elimination of garbage as a bear attraction through use of protective holding facilities, followed by timely removal and adequate disposal.

(a) Use of bear-proof garbage cans throughout the Park.

(b) Use of incinerators at Sperry and Granite Park Chalets and at St. Mary, and elimination of outside garbage dumps.

(c) Adoption of regulations prohibiting bear feeding by visitors, thereby minimizing the opportunities for bears to become positively conditioned to the presence of unnatural foods.

(d) Use of modern vehicular garbage-carrying equipment to make frequent pick-ups and eliminate overnight carry-over of garbage.

(e) Establishment of regulations requiring all back country users to carry out their own litter and garbage, the so-called "Pack-in, Pack-out" policy of the Park.

(3) Placement of limitations on use of trails and backcountry areas.

(a) Temporary closures of trails and backcountry areas or restrictions on camping and hiking when there has been a sighting or confrontation with a sow and her cubs; also frequent sightings of a grizzly at or near a trail may be cause for its closure.

(b) Follow-up checks by ranger personnel in such areas to determine the extent of the problem, and the date when limitations may safely be removed.

(c) Enforcement of backcountry restrictions through ranger patrol and otherwise.

(4) Relocation of nuisance bears to more remote areas, and destruction of animals proving to be incorrigible. Park Service statistics for the period 1946-1970 show that a total of 25 grizzlies were destroyed, representing an average of one per year for the quarter of a century involved. Of these 25, 13 were in backcountry areas, and the other 12 in developed areas. Five others were transplanted to distant areas where, hopefully, they could start a new life.

(5) Respecting of grizzly habitats by the scheduling of no new trails in the wilder areas.

(6) Ecological evaluations of present and proposed trails, camp-sites and other facilities to provide guidelines for preventive management.

Follow-Through By Authorities

Enforcement has been stressed as an essential part of the program. Visitors apprehended in the act of feeding bears are brought before the United States magistrate and fined. Likewise, the "Pack-in, Pack-out" policy is being enforced on the backcountry trails. Horse and foot patrol by ranger personnel is part of a program to keep the back country clean; also assigned to backcountry patrol have been other rangers with special qualifications, such as a degree in ecology. Trail crews are charged with the responsibility for cleaning up any campground debris and picking up roadside litter.

At Park Headquarters grizzly sightings are kept track of on a daily basis, with computer printouts being sent by telecopier to ranger stations and visitor centers. A check is also maintained on black bears seen. Warnings are posted and trails are closed, as a rule, after sightings of a sow with cubs, after injuries to Park visitors, after reports of carrion along the trail, or after aggressive confrontation with any bear. Nuisance bears are captured by two-man (or more) crews using a tranquilizer gun, then are transported by helicopter to a remote backcountry location while still in a temporarily immobilized condition. Handling the problem bear effectively represents a very important part of the over-all program for handling the bear problem.

The well-conceived Park Service program to bring the grizzly problem under control has been paying valuable dividends, making it possible to achieve substantial compliance with the congressional mandate that our parks be preserved in their natural state, *unimpaired for the enjoyment of future generations.*

What Of The Future?

Since the yearly total of Park visitors is now well over 1,500,000, largely concentrated in the brief summer season, continued increases in annual visitation figures are predictable, and additional controls may become necessary. A more restrictive program of assignment and control of overnight capacity in backcountry areas through camping permits may be imposed; also there may be area restrictions to certain kinds or times of travel, special fishing regulations to reduce the attractiveness of fish odors, with perhaps a consideration of alternatives to transplanting nuisance grizzlies within Park boundaries. Action to control the number of grizzlies themselves may become necessary, although no such plans are currently under consideration.

Some observers are of the opinion that the growth in Park visitation figures may be only one reason for the difficulty in exercising complete control of the bear problem. They also feel that, owing to extremely favorable conditions in the Park, it is likely that the grizzly birthrate has been regularly exceeding the number of deaths (few from other than natural causes,) thereby bringing the grizzly population close to the saturation point, and perhaps beyond it in certain areas. If their theory is correct, and the areas of over-crowding happen to coincide with those of high visitor density, confrontations will be inevitable. They suggest that when this is found to be the case, not only should preventive measures be taken as at present, but the problem bears should be sought out and dealt with summarily before they have a chance to maim or kill.

Whatever the explanation, the events of 1976 have made it apparent that the new threat posed by the adolescent, or sub-adult, grizzly is serious and will require intensive study. It may be trite to say that every happening has its cause, if it can only be discovered; nevertheless, it would appear that a solution for this new and puzzling development will depend upon achieving an understanding of the reason or reasons behind the activities of these young and hitherto non-troublesome animals. The need for such an early understanding and for preventive action based upon it is urgent.

Reprinted from

Papers and Proceedings
Rapports et Procès-verbaux

THIRD INTERNATIONAL CONFERENCE

ON

Bears

—Their Biology and Management

BINGHAMTON, NEW YORK, U.S.A.

and

MOSCOW, U.S.S.R.

June 1974

Union Internationale
pour la Conservation de la Nature
et de ses Ressources

International Union
for Conservation of Nature
and Natural Resources

Morges, Switzerland, 1976

Paper 13

Ecological Role and Management of Grizzly Bears in Glacier National Park, Montana

C. J. MARTINKA
Glacier National Park, West Glacier, Montana 59936.

INTRODUCTION

Colonization of western North America by modern man led to significant reduction in numbers and distribution of grizzly bears, *Ursus arctos,* during the
past 150 years (Storer & Trevis 1955). Response has been classically evident
south of Canada where widespread population declines and local extinctions
have occurred. Viable populations have persisted only in more expansive
wilderness and park areas of Montana and Wyoming where remoteness and
land use characteristics contribute to their protection. National parks provide
unique refugia where the natural integrity of grizzly bears can be preserved
as an ecosystem component by mitigating detrimental effects of modern man.

This paper summarizes current knowledge relating to the ecological role and
management of grizzly bears in Glacier National Park, Montana. The park is
administered as a natural area within which grizzlies require a spectrum of
management considerations. These may be broadly categorized as environmental requirements and relationships to park visitors. Field studies of population biology and ecosystem relationships provide criteria for interpretation
of environmental requirements within park ecosystems (Martinka 1972; 1974a).
Evaluations of management programs contribute to an understanding of relationships between grizzlies and park visitors (Martinka 1971; 1974b).

HISTORICAL PERSPECTIVE

Evaluation of species evolution permits a more complete understanding of
current status since adaptive development can frequently be correlated with
changing environments. These changes may occur within established geo-
graphic ranges or result from emigration to new areas. In the case of grizzly
bears, physical and behavioral adaptations associated with speciation resulted
in potentially efficient utilization of a variety of habitats. In contrast, ability
to cope with certain associated fauna may have been less pronounced. Current
status and relationships in North America reflect a number of traits which
developed during the evolutionary process.

Paleontological records suggest that the grizzly bear differentiated from the
Etruscan bear, *Ursus etruscus,* in Asia during the middle Pleistocene (Thenius
1959; Kurten 1968; Herrero 1972). Speciation occurred during a time when
climatic fluctuations caused periodically extensive glaciation in northern continental areas. Extensive replacement of forests with treeless tundra and
steppe accompanied cold phases and glacial maxima (Giterman & Golubeva
1967). Adaptation to the presence of these treeless habitats appears to have
been a key element associated with genetic separation of the grizzly from its
forestdwelling ancestor (Herrero 1972).

Formation of land bridges during glacial maxima provided opportunities for
faunal interchange between Asia and North America. Dispersals were pre-

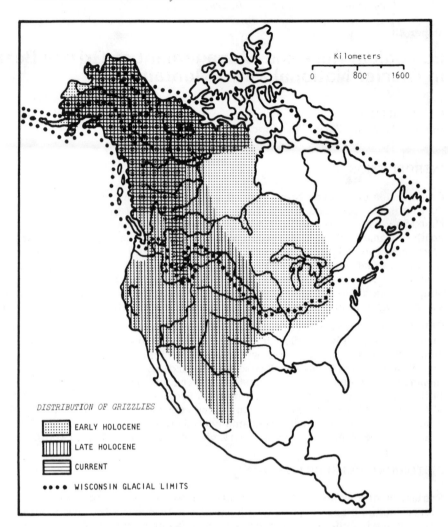

F ig. 1.   Postglacial distribution of grizzly bears in North America.

dominantly eastward and generally included species adapted to forest environments during the early and middle Pleistocene (Repenning 1967). Steppe and
tundra forms dominated late dispersals and it appears that grizzlies did not
successfully colonize Alaska until the Wisconsin glacial period (Herrero 1972).
Continued range expansion was temporarily restricted at that point by the
merged Cordilleran and Laurentide ice sheets.

Recession of the continental ice sheets opened extensive areas of suitable
habitat for grizzly bears in North America (Figure 1). Distribution expanded
eastward to Ontario (Peterson 1965), Ohio and Kentucky (Guilday 1968), and
southward into Mexico (Storer & Trevis 1955). Distributional recession
apparently followed eastward expansion in response to development of un-
favourable environmental conditions (Guilday 1968). Populations were present
throughout most of western North America during the eighteenth century
(Storer & Trevis 1955), but the rapidity of local extinctions suggests that many
of these were also of marginal status.

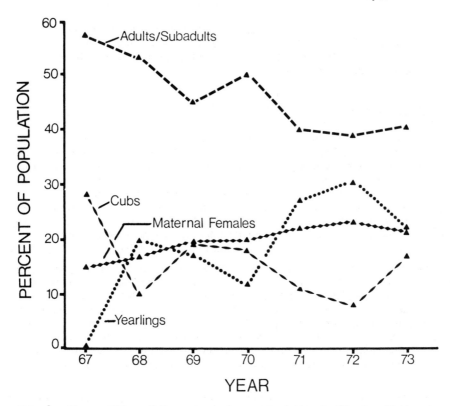

Fig. 2. Composition of the grizzly bear population in Glacier National Park as determined from annual classification of different bears from 1967 through 1973.

Present distribution of grizzlies is largely restricted to the more secure mountain habitats of northwestern North America (Figure 1). It seems likely that postglacial occupancy progressed from midcontinental habitats as mountain glaciers receded and food sources developed. Mosaics of forest, grasslands, and alpine tundra provided a productive habitat for grizzlies but also reintroduced potential competition with black bears, *Ursus americanus*. This closely related species had dispersed to North America during an earlier period and was well adapted to forest environments.

Primitive man and grizzly bears apparently occupied North America in a biologically neutral relationship. In contrast, relatively recent emigration of modern man to North America added a significant dimension to the postglacial history of the grizzly. Protection of human life, depredation control. sport hunting and habitat deterioration were focal points which contributed to population declines. These pressures continue to the present but public expressions have recently added a protective phase to the history of grizzly bears.

Significant developments in the relationship between modern man and grizzly bears are reflected in the history of Glacier National Park. Grizzlies were encountered and shot when railroad survey parties first entered the area in the mid 1800s (Stevens 1860; Pumpelley 1918). Faunal richness attracted sport hunters during the late 1800s (Schultz 1962) and by 1900 commercial trapping of the bears for hides was a common activity (Bailey & Bailey 1918). These activities undoubtedly influenced grizzly populations until establishment of the park in 1910 provided protection. Limited control continued thereafter but of insufficient magnitude to prevent restoration of a natural grizzly bear population (Martinka 1971; 1974a).

POPULATION STATUS

Glacier is presently inhabited by a wild grizzly bear population which ranges throughout the park under essentially natural conditions. Population estimates determined from density samples ranged from 175-230 and averaged 191 for 7 years of study from 1967-73. Annual fluctuations resulted from deficiencies in the census technique but general trends suggest that population levels were relatively stable. Regulation of numbers is thought to occur naturally through social interaction and associated dispersal and/or death of subordinate bears. Aging of hunter-killed bears and depredation controls beyond the park's periphery provide tentative support for this hypothesis (Greer 1971; 1972; 1974).

The population is characteristically structured as single individuals and family groups (Martinka 1974a). Annual classifications of different bears observed showed means of 46, 20, 16 and 18 percent unclassified adults, productive females, cubs, and yearlings, respectively (Figure 2). Trends toward increasing proportions of maternal females and their offspring correlated with decreasing proportions of unclassified adults observed during the study. Substantial fluctuations occurred in annual production of cubs but combined proportions of cubs and yearlings exhibited a trend similar to that of maternal females.

The mean increment of 16 percent cubs contributed approximately 31 potentially new members to the population each year. Realized recruitment appeared contrastingly low in view of stable population trends and apparent longevity of adult bears (Greer 1971; 1972; 1974; Mundy & Flook 1973). Recruitment probably relates to a replacement function involving displacement and/or mortality of established population members. Surplus subadults likely succumbed to mortality through social interactions, emigrated to vacant habitats, or both.

An average density of 4.6 grizzlies per 100 km^2 was computed from the mean population estimate of 191 bears. Exclusion of offspring provides a basis for estimating a potential breeding density of 2.9 bears per 100 km^2. The presence of sexually immature subadults could reasonably reduce effective breeding densities to 2.5 bears per 100 km^2. This low density requires compensatory movement patterns to assure adequate gene flow and prevent the potential influence of genetic drift on isolated population segments (Wilson & Bossert 1971). The complexity of these patterns is suggested by Craighead & Craighead (1965), Martinka (1970), Mundy & Flook (1973), Murie (1944, 1961) and Pearson (1972).

ECOLOGICAL NICHE

Glacier National Park encompasses 4100 km^2 of cordilleran terrain in northwestern Montana. Glaciation has created rugged topography which is extensively occupied by coniferous forests at lower elevations and alpine tundra above the timberline. Wildfire and snowslides provide habitat diversity within coniferous forests by maintaining seral shrub and conifer communities. Local influences of soil and wind on certain sites have contributed to the formation of grasslands. Combinations of terrain and vegetation provide an interspersed array of habitats for the grizzly bear population.

Each of the major habitats was utilized by grizzlies during the May through October period of activity. Frequent use was made of coniferous forests but a distinct preference was apparent for treeless types. Grasslands and tundra provided relatively permanent open habitats while wildfire and snowslides created favorable types within the coniferous forest zone. Movements to higher elevation shrub and alpine habitats occurred during the snowfree summer and early fall season. Bears were most consistently observed in areas of maximum habitat diversity.

Seasonal progression in habitat use was accompanied by a predictable sequence in the predominantly herbivorous diet. Spring and early summer preferences included grasses, Gramineae, horsetail, *Equisetem* spp., and cowparsnip, *Heracleum lanatum*. Ripening fruits of huckleberry, *Vaccinium* spp., supplemented with serviceberry, *Amelanchier* spp., mountain ash, *Sorbus scopulina,* and hawthorne, *Crategus* spp., formed the bulk of late summer and fall diets. Predation, scavenging, and digging occasionally added variety in the form of mammals, roots and insects.

Food habits reveal that the grizzly is well adapted to efficient utilization of postglacial mountain habitats. An obvious preference for certain herbaceous foods displaced potential use of numerous alternative items which were also present. Food abundance and distribution undoubtedly influence densities to some extent. For example, ample foods have apparently permitted development of a high density potential by coastal populations in Alaska (Troyer & Hensel 1964). Contrasting conditions existed on historic steppe and tundra habitats where herbaceous foods were widely scattered or in limited supply. Foraging by predation, scavenging and digging most likely evolved under these conditions. The population in Glacier seems to be regulated at a point somewhat below the biomass carrying capacity of the habitat.

Seasonally high densities of grizzlies are occasionally observed in Glacier. An area of particular interest includes 22 km^2 of high elevation seral shrub habitat on the Apgar Mountains which was created by a wildfire in 1929. The relatively dependable huckleberry crops produced on the area each year attract bears when fruit production fails in surrounding habitats. Combined aerial and ground observations in 1967 and 1973 revealed that late summer densities reached as high as 1.3 grizzlies per km^2 under these conditions (Table 1). Spacing was distinct among the social units present with one agonistic interaction recorded involving an adult chasing a subadult. High concentrations continued for several weeks but the temporary, unpredictable and local nature of the phenomenon reduced potential as a significant influence on overall population levels.

A late summer concentration of black bears also occurred on the Apgar Mountains. The magnitude of observed densities was inversely related to numbers of grizzlies present (Table 2). A low density of grizzlies in 1967 apparently permitted foraging by numerous black bears in spaced distribution. In contrast, a high density of grizzlies in 1973 nearly precluded use by black bears. Those observed were in distinct association with forest edges or isolated stands.

The significance of forest canopies to the evolution of both species has been discussed by Herrero (1972). Highly developed arboreal capabilities by black bears apparently contribute to competitive superiority in forest habitats.

147

TABLE 1. DENSITY ESTIMATES FOR GRIZZLY BEARS ON A 22 KM² AREA
OF THE APGAR MOUNTAINS DURING LATE SUMMER AS
DETERMINED FROM COMBINED EVALUATION OF AERIAL AND
GROUND SIGHTINGS OF DIFFERENT BEARS IN 1967 AND 1973.

| | Type of Sightings | | | | Total Number of Different Grizzlies | Bears per Square Kilometer |
| | Aerial 1/ | | Ground 2/ | | | |
Year	Adults	Young	Adults	Young		
1967	7	2	1	2	12	0.5
1973	5	7	9	7	28	1.3

1/ One hour helicopter survey plus routine sightings during management
flights.

2/ Associated primarily with fire surviellance and/or suppression activities.

TABLE 2. GRIZZLY AND BLACK BEARS OBSERVED DURING 1 HOUR
HELICOPTER FLIGHTS IN A 22 KM² AREA OF APGAR
MOUNTAINS DURING SEPTEMBER OF 1967 AND 1973.

| | Number of Different Bears Observed | |
Year	Grizzlies	Black Bears
1967	9	16
1973	20	6

Aggressiveness and extended maternal care provide competitive advantages
for grizzlies in open habitats. Interspecies relationships have apparently
evolved to a point of mutual avoidance where spacing is maintained. This
system permits overlap in habitat use and is an important consideration in
determining population levels of both species.

MANAGEMENT OF GRIZZLIES

Current management is directed toward the dual objectives of park visitor
protection and maintenance of a natural grizzly bear population. Field management procedures include a visitor information program, control of attractive
unnatural foods, opportunity for visitor travel restrictions, and removal of
persistently troublesome bears. Annual program evaluation considers number
of conflicts and management actions relative to trends in visitation. Results
for 1968 through 1973 are presented in Table 3.

Progressive increases in park visitation through 1973 were accompanied by
generally low encounter rates between bears and visitors. Those which
occurred were predominantly aggressive displays or equipment damages.
Increased contacts during 1972 and 1973 correlated with rapid expansion of
backcountry use by hikers and campers. Management response through temporary travel restrictions apparently mitigated the potential for human in-

TABLE 3. SUMMARY OF VISITATION, GRIZZLY BEAR CONFRONTATIONS WITH VISITORS, AND MANAGEMENT ACTIONS IN GLACIER NATIONAL PARK, 1968 THROUGH 1973.

Year	Annual Visitation			Grizzly Bear Confrontations		Management Action		
	Total 1/	Overnight Visits 2/		Belligerent Encounter	Personal Injuries	Visitor Restrictions	Transplant	Disposal
		Campgrounds and Hotels	Backcountry 3/					
1968	936,000	366,000	8,000	5	1	6	0	2
1969	1,023,000	337,000	10,000	2	0	5	0	3
1970	1,034,000	328,000	10,000	0	0	1	1	0
1971	1,081,000	328,000	15,000	3	0	7	1	0
1972	1,114,000	326,000	22,000	12	0	9	1	0
1973	1,174,000	337,000	32,000	7	0	9	0	1

1/ Total visitors passing through gates one or more times, adjusted to exclude those on transient access route.

2/ Visits defined as one visitor for one day in each category.

3/ Includes two chalets.

juries. In addition, bear control was maintained at a biologically acceptable rate for a natural area.

Mutual avoidance appears to be a key element in current relationships between grizzly bears and park visitors. Management design and characteristic shyness of bears are the principal factors contributing to an essentially compatible coexistence. Effects of the relationship on visitors are measureable in terms of imposed changes in activity patterns and travel distributions. Response by grizzlies is more difficult to document but observations suggest that population dynamics and ecosystem role remain nearly unaltered from pristine conditions.

Projections of management needs characteristically identify additional control of human activities as a primary goal (Martinka 1974b). However, it is becoming increasingly apparent that certain ecological phenomena may also require consideration. The potential significance of wildfire seems particularly important as demonstrated by its ability to cause extensive structural and compositional change in park habitats. Temporary reduction or elimination of forest canopies appears to create superior habitat for the grizzly. In contrast, successional advance toward mature forests creates conditions more favorable for black bears. The latter trend has been enhanced by a wildfire suppression policy which continues to the present. Restoration of wildfire to its natural ecosystem role is considered essential to maintaining a natural grizzly bear population within the park.

A wild, free-ranging population of grizzly bears has been shown to present the least conflict with visitors in Glacier National Park (Martinka 1971). Prudent application of facts to management planning is required to assure continued low conflict rates and protect the natural integrity of the bear population.

REFERENCES

BAILEY, V. and BAILEY, F. M. 1918. *Wild animals of Glacier National Park.* Washington, D.C., U.S. Government Printing Office. 210pp.

CRAIGHEAD, F. C., Jr. and CRAIGHEAD, J. J. 1965. Tracking grizzly bears. *BioScience,* 15 (2): 88-92.

GITERMAN, R. E. and GOLUBEVA, L. V. 1967. Vegetation of eastern Siberia during the Anthropogene Period. In D. M. Hopkins ed., *The Bering land bridge.* Stanford University Press, Stanford, Calif. Pp. 232-244.

GREER, K. R. 1971. Big game research, wildlife laboratory. *Montana Fish and Game Department Job Completion Rept.,* P.-R. Project W-120-R-2 35pp. Multilith.

GREER, K. R. 1972. Grizzly bear mortality and management programs in Montana during 1971. *Montana Fish and Game Department Job Completion Rept.,* P.-R. Project W-120-R-4. 30pp. Multilith.

GREER, K. R. 1974. Grizzly bear mortality and management programs in Montana during 1972. *Montana Fish and Game Department Job Completion Rept.,* P.-R. Project W-120-R-4. 30pp. Multilith.

GUILDAY, J. E. 1968. Grizzly bears from eastern North America. *Amer. Midland Naturalist* 79 (1): 247-250.

HERRERO, S. 1972. Aspects of evolution and adaptation in American black bears (*Ursus americanus* Pallas) and brown and grizzly bears (*U. arctos* Linné) of North America. In S. Herrero, ed., *Bears—Their biology and management.* Morges, IUCN New Series **23**: 221-231.

KURTEN, B. 1968. *Pleistocene mammals of Europe.* The world naturalist series. London, Weidenfeld and Nicolson. 317pp.

MARTINKA, C. J. 1970. Grizzly ecology studies, Glacier National Park, *National Park Service Prog. Rept.,* 1969. 43pp. (xerox).

MARTINKA, C. J. 1971. Status and management of grizzly bears in Glacier National Park, Montana. *Trans. N. Am. Wildl. and Nat. Resour. Conf.,* **36**: 312-322.

MARTINKA, C. J. 1972. Habitat relationships of grizzly bears in Glacier National Park, Montana. *National Park Service Progress Rept.* 19pp. (xerox).

MARTINKA, C. J. 1974a. Population characteristics of grizzly bears in Glacier National Park, Montana. *J. Mamm.* **55** (1): 21-29.

MARTINKA, C. J. 1974b. Preserving the natural status of grizzlies in Glacier National Park. *Wildl. Soc. Bull.* **2** (1): 13-17.

MUNDY, K. R. D. and FLOOK, D. R. 1973 Background for managing grizzly bears in the national parks of Canada. *Canadian Wildlife Ser. Rept.* Series **22**:1-36.

MURIE, A. 1944. The wolves of Mt. McKinley. *United States National Park Ser. Fauna Series* **5**. 238pp.

MURIE, A. 1961. *A naturalist in Alaska.* Devin-Adair Co., New York 302pp.

PEARSON, A. M. 1972. Population characteristics of the northern interior grizzly in the Yukon Territory, Canada. In S. Herrero ed., *Bears—Their biology and management.* Morges, IUCN New Series **23**:32-35.

PETERSON, R. L. 1965. A well-preserved grizzly bear skull recovered from a late glacial deposit near Lake Simcoe, Ontario. *Nature* **208** (5016): 1233-1234.

PUMPELLY, R. 1918. *Reminiscences.* New York, N.Y., Henry Holt and Company, 2 vols. 844pp.

REPENNING, C. A. 1967. Palearctic—Nearctic mammalian dispersals in the late Cenozoic. In D. M. Hopkins ed., *The Bering land bridge.* Stanford, Calif., Stanford University Press. Pp. 288-311.

SCHULTZ, J. W. 1962. *Blackfeet and buffalo—memories of life among the Indians.* Norman, Okla., University of Oklahoma Press. 384pp.

STEVENS, S. I. 1860. Explorations for a route for a Pacific railroad, near the forty-seventh and forty-ninth parallels of north latitude, from St. Paul to Puget Sound. In *Reports of explorations and surveys to ascertain the most practical and economical route for a railroad from the Mississippi River to the Pacific Ocean XII (1).* Washington, D.C., Thomas H. Ford, Printer. 358pp

STORER, T. I. and TREVIS, L. P. 1955. *California grizzly.* Berkeley, University of California Press. 355pp.

THENIUS, E. 1959. Ursidenphylogenese und biostatigraphie. *Zeitschr. Säugertierkunde* **24**:78-84.

TROYER, W. A. and HENSEL, R. J. 1964. Structure and distribution of a Kodiak bear population. *J. Wildl. Mgmt.* **28** (4):769-772.

WILSON, E. O. and BOSSERT, W. H. 1971. *A primer of population biology.* Stanford, Conn., Sinaur Associates Inc. 192pp.

INDEX

Adams, James Capen, 19, 59, 71, 72, 74
A-koch-kit-ope, 95, 96,
Alaska, 24, 43, 49
American Natural History, 59
Anti-Grizzly View, 127
Anza expedition, 26
Arctic Canada, 43
Ascension, Father, 25
Aspeslet, Malcolm, 49
Assiniboine River, 27
Audubon, John J., 48

Badger Creek, 83
Bailey, Vernon, 3, 49
Balu Pass, 49
Baring family, 2
Barnum museum, 74
Barnum, Phineas T., 73, 74
Bear problems, 11
Beck, Barb, 99
Beebe, "Chance," 97
Bessie, Mr., 65-67
"Big Plains Grizzly," 1, 47
Black Hills, 3, 32
Black, Roscoe, 10
Blackfoot Basin, 79
Boulder Pass, 98
Bowman, Eldon G., 129
Brackenridge, 46
British Columbia, 7, 30
Broadway, New York, 74
Bunney, Gary, 119

California, 30, 65, 73
California Menagerie, 73, 74
Camas Lake trail, 6
Canada, 4
Canadian Wildlife Service, 7
Caras, Roger, 130
Cardston, Alberta, 113
Carson, Kit, 58
Cascade Mountains, 24
Charlevoix, Pierre de, 28
Charlton, Massachusetts, 74
Chopunnish Indians, 38
Clark, Captain, 33, 36, 39
Clark, Malcolm, 58
Climber's Guide to Glacier National Park, 105
Clinton, De Witt, 46, 48
Colorado, 24, 65, 76
Colorado Rockies, 75
Columbia River, 37, 51
Columbus, 41
Coppermine River, 28
Craighead brothers, 135

Cram, J. Harold, 83, 85, 86
Cranbrook, British Columbia, 7
Cree Indians, 4
Custer, General, 3
Custer's massacre, 77
Cut Bank Pass, 89
Cut Bank Valley, 60, 89, 97
Cutright, Paul Russell, 62

Daily Inter Lake, 127
Dakotas, 24, 40
Dakotas, grizzlies in, 31
Dawson Pass, 88
Denver Zoo, 71
De Smet, Father Pierre J., 48, 51, 52, 58
Devereau, Joan, 119
Drewyer, killed grizzly, 37
Drummond, botanist, 59
Ducat, Roy, 118, 119
Dunn, Paul, 120, 122

Edwards, J. Gordon, 105

Fages, Lieutenant, 26
Feather Plume Falls, 105
Femmes Fatales, 99
Fishercap Lake, 10
Flathead River, 5, 6, 7
Fort Benton, 2
Fort Churchill, 7
Fort Mandan, 32
Fox, H.A., 77
Franklin, Ben, 72
Future Park Service plans, 139

Game protection, 4
Garbage dumps, 5
George, Jean, 130
Giefer Creek, Grizzly of, 7
Glacier Park, 1, 4, 7, 24, 27, 49, 50, 60, 63, 71, 75, 89, 99, 107, 115, 116, 117, 127, 133, 134, 135, 136
Glacier Park, B.C., 99
Glacier Park, fatalities by grizzlies, 11
Glacier Park, 1976 season, 9
Glass, Hugh, 58
Goathaunt, 10
Godboldt, James, 111
Going-to-the-Sun Camp, 6
Going-to-the-Sun Highway, 10
Golden Fleece, 73
Granite Park, 9, 118, 119, 120
Great Northern Railway, 76, 83, 101, 102, 103
Grinnell, George Bird, 2, 75, 76, 78, 100, 107
Grisly, 45

Grizzlies,
  As pets, 65
  Coat and coloring, 14
  Comparison with black bears, 13
  Cubhood and maturity, 17
  Day-to-day routine, 21
  Ferocity, 57
  Foods and feeding, 22
  General physique, 15
  Hibernation, 22, 23
  Longevity and death, 16
  Not gregarious, 52
  Number of, in Park, 4
  Origin of names, 43, 44
  Physical characteristics, 14
  Range covered, 24
  Removal of, 7, 138
  Sagacity and dignity, 20
  Sightings of, 5
  Size and weight, 16
  Speed and strength, 16
  Tenacity of life, 54, 55, 56
  Various misbeliefs, 53
Grizzly, king of game animals, 19
Grizzly myths, 51
Grizzly program, 133, 137, 138
Grizzly, the bear's viewpoint, 62
Gulliver era, 25

Hansen, Dr. Wilmer C., 115
Harte, Bret, 65
Hearne, Samuel, 28, 44
Hegelsen, Julie, 22, 23
Hidden Lake, 9, 60
Highline trail, 9
Hittell, Theodore H., 71, 73
"Hohhost" grizzly, 38
Hornaday, Dr. W.T., 59
Hough, Emerson, 2
Huckle, Denise, 120
Hudson Bay, 27, 44, 51
Hudson's Bay Company, 27, 48
Hungry Horse News, 127

Iceberg Lake, 9
Idaho, 29
Introductory Discourse, 46

Jackson Glacier, 77
Jackson, Robert, 2, 3
Jackson, William, 2, 3, 76, 89
Jefferson, Thomas, 31
Jim, Miss, 65, 66
Johnny and Jenny, 68-71
Johnson, Dr. James, 114
Josephine Lake, 106

Kalispell, 6
Kansas, 24
Kelsey, Henry, 27
Kintla Lake, 4
Kogler, Thomas, 7
Koons, Michele, 120, 122
Koontz, Roy, 7

Lady Washington, 71, 74
Lahontan, Baron, 27
Lake McDonald Lodge, 5
Landseer Edwin, 48
Lewis and Clark, 13, 15, 31, 37, 39, 40, 45, 46, 49, 54, 58, 60, 62, 63
Lewis and Clark Forest Reserve, 4
Lewis, Meriwether, 31-33, 35, 36, 40, Old Ephraim, 44, 51
Little Big Horn, 3, 77
Logan Pass, 4, 9
Logging Lake, 9
Long, Stephen T., 48
Louisiana Purchase, 311

MacKenzie, Alexander, 29, 45
Many Glacier Campground, 10
Many Glacier Hotel, 5, 106, 111, 112
Many Glacier Ranger Station, 10
Marias Pass, 7
Martinka, Clifford J., 50, 135, 136
McClintock, Walter, 89-91, 97
McCracken, Harold, 28
McDonald Lake, 118, 121, 122, 127
Medicine Bow Mountains, 67
Medicine Grizzly, 96, 97
Medicine Grizzly Lake, 97
Medicine Grizzly Legend, 93-96
Medicine Grizzly Peak, 97
Meek, Joe, 58
Merced River, 72
Merriam, Dr. C. Hart, 49
Mexico City, 24
Mills, Enos, 13, 18, 20, 63, 68-71
Miss Grizzly, 67-68
Mission to the Kilistinouc, 27
Mississippi River, 34
Missouri River, 1, 32, 37, 39, 40
Moment, Gairdner, 117
Monroe, Hugh, 2, 89
Monroe, Hugh, 2, 89
Montana, 24, 32, 38, 40, 76, 77, 78,
Montana Rockies, 87
Montana State University, 10, 135
Monterey Bay, 25
Montez, Lola, 65
Mountaineer Museum, 72, 73
Muir, John, 19, 20, 58
Munroe, 77, 78, 79, 83, 85
Mt. Jackson, 79
Mt. Penrose, 104
Mt. Stanton, 121
My Vacations, 75, 86

National Park Service, 7, 11, 127, 130, Saskatchewan, 27
Nebraska, 24

Nelson, Alan, 107-111, 113, 114
New World bears, 25
Nez Perce Indians, 38, 43
Noring, Greta, 108-110, 112-114
North Dakota, 32, 49
Noseck, Ron and Ray, 120, 122
Nuisance bears, 138
Nyack, 103, 104
Nyhlen, Gote, 108-111

Odyssey, American, 39
Okotomi Lake, 107
Old Ephraim, 44, 51
Old North Trail, 89
Old Rory, 77-81
Ord, George, 46-48, 58, 63
Oregon, 67
Oregon Missions, 51
Outerbridge, Frank, 83

Pacific Coast, 24
Pacific Museum, 73
Parratt, Smith, 107-116
Peace River, 29
Peale's Museum, 48
Pennant, Thomas, 28, 45
Penrose, Boies, 101
Penrose, Dr. Charles B., 100
"Perils of Pauline," 40
Pike, Zebulon, 48
Pinchot, Amos, 77
Pinchot, Gifford, 77
Pinchot brothers, 83
Portola, Gaspar de, 26
Pro-Grizzly view, 128
Pulitzer, Ralph, 2
Putnam, A.W., 77, 83

Questions raised, 122, 123, 125, 127

Rambler, a greyhound, 72
Rescue Creek, 104
Reese, Dr. Lewis, 111, 112
Rising Sun Campground, 107, 108, 111
Rising Wolf Mountain, 2
Rocky Mountains, 24 38, 48, 59, 68
Rocky Mountain goat, 2, 14
Rocky Mountain grizzly, 1
Rocky Mountain sheep, 2, 32, 90
Rogue bears, 5, 6
Rollins, Philip, 66
Roop, Larry, 135
Roosevelt, Theodore, 19, 20, 44, 49, 58,
Russell, Andy, 117, 129

Sacajawea, 39, 40
Sampson, 72, 73, 74
San Francisco, 26, 72, 73
San Francisco Midwinter Fair, 19
San Luis Obispo, 26
Saskatchewan, 27
Say, T., 48

Schultz, James Willard, 2, 77
Seventh Cvalry, 77
Seward, Willaim H., Jr., 76
"Show Time" at hotels, 5
Sierra Nevada Mountains, 24, 71
Siksikakoan, 89-91, 93, 96-97
Singleshot Mountain, 2
Smithsonian Institution, 49
Squirt, 121
Steamboat Springs, 75
Steep Trails, 58
Stevenson, Donald, 15
Stiles, A.L., 101, 102, 105
Stimpson, Henry L., 2, 75-87
Stimpson's sister, 77, 84
St. Louis, 31
St. Mary area, 3
St. Mary Lake, 6, 75, 76, 77
St. Mary Ranger Station, 111
St. Mary River, 76
St. Mary Village, 10
Stoney Indian Pass, 10
Summit, 4
Swiftcurrent Pass, 118
Swiftcurrent Valley, 2

Taft, President, 75
Tales of the Argonauts, 65
Territorial imperative, 20
"Threatened species," 8
Triple Divide Pass, 89
Trout Lake, 118, 121, 122, 125, 128
Two Medicine Lake, 2, 88, 89
Two Medicine valley, 2

Umfreville, Edward, 29, 45, 51, 52
University of Montana, 10
Ursus arctos, 49, 50
Ursus horribilis, 46, 47, 49, 117
U.S. Geological Survey, 101, 104, 105

Valle, a French trader, 32
Vandalism, 6
Viviparous Quadrupeds of North America 48
Vizcaino, Captain, 25

Washington, 24, 71
Waterton Lake, 10
Whale Creek, 7
White bear, 32, 40, 43
Wigwam Creek, 7
Winnipeg, 27
Winthrop, Bronson, 77
Wright, William H., 55, 59-63, 97
Wyoming, 24, 65, 67

Yellowstone Park, 1, 24, 63, 127, 133, 13
Yellowstone River, 32, 38, 39
Yosemite Valley, 19, 20